HOW TO GET AHEAD IN LIFE

Hidden Secrets of the Rich

by

Anthony Winston

The contents of this work, including, but not limited to, the accuracy of events, people, and places depicted; opinions expressed; permission to use previously published materials included; and any advice given or actions advocated are solely the responsibility of the author, who assumes all liability for said work and indemnifies the publisher against any claims stemming from publication of the work.

All Rights Reserved
Copyright © 2015 by Anthony Winston

No part of this book may be reproduced or transmitted, downloaded, distributed, reverse engineered, or stored in or introduced into any information storage and retrieval system, in any form or by any means, including photocopying and recording, whether electronic or mechanical, now known or hereinafter invented without permission in writing from the publisher.

Dorrance Publishing Co
585 Alpha Drive
Suite 103
Pittsburgh, PA 15238
Visit our website at *www.dorrancebookstore.com*

ISBN: 978-1-4809-1974-7
eISBN: 978-1-4809-2089-7

How to Get Rich and Get Ahead in Life

Why should we strive to become rich? All that becoming rich means is that we want a fuller and more abundant life. It is striving to become the best people we can be. To not want abundance and wealth is not normal, and that person has convinced himself to settle.

Becoming rich can help with the most important commodity we have – time. So, instead of cleaning your house on a Saturday morning, you can pay someone to do it and enjoy the things you truly want to do such as golf, travel, reading, spending time with your children, etc. Become rich so that you can do kind things, visit distant lands, educate yourself, or help the world find the truth for our existence.

The key to helping others is to first help yourself so that you can lead others and teach them how to "fish" and help themselves so that they may then help others. In other words: you need to make the most of yourself. A great quote from Franklin D. Roosevelt states, "Happiness is not in the mere possession of money, it lies in the joy of achievement, in the thrill of creative effort."

Let's start out with some statistics because after I show them to you, I really believe that by learning some of the skills in this book, you can become one of the good stats. In a Nielson study, almost 25% of our population has zero cash left after they pay their basic bills. Only the top one percent have an annual income of over $364,000. The top .01 percent earn over $5.5 million. Sixty percent of Americans earn less than $69,000. The median household income is less than $49,000 as of 2009.

Education has a great deal to do with it. But even those who are well educated rarely have wealth. Eighty percent of Americans earn less than $80,000. So if you do not want to be like 80% of Americans, do not do what 80% of Americans do!

Average Americans do not typically own their own business. 82% of NFL athletes lose their savings and file for bankruptcy within two years of their last game. With salaries and wages such as these, the average American cannot afford college or even to save for retirement. Also, by nature it takes hard work. If you can truly look into your heart and know that you are a hard worker then you can easily become rich.

You might just be spending your energy doing the wrong thing because you do not know any better. It's like a caveman feverishly rubbing sticks together to build a fire when you can do it in two seconds by lighting a match. If you truly know that you are not a hard worker, then you have work to do on your mentality.

Yes, it can be taught, but it has to be the hardest section of the book to do. The techniques are listed here for you to change your thought process. So changes have to be made, and through this book I truly believe if you are that average American, working through some of the techniques and a way of thinking supplied here, you can truly achieve wealth.

Why are most people not millionaires? One reason is because they do not think it is possible, so they stop before they even get started. That is why I focus a great deal of attention on the mentality section. It has to be a goal to become financially independent. If it is not, then you will not become rich. (I am assuming you are not one of those people since you bought this book.) The fact is that if someone else has achieved the level of success you are looking for, it is evidence that you can do the same.

As of now your thoughts about money came from your parents. If your parents thought money was tight, that life was a struggle and money was hard to come by, you no doubt picked up on some of these beliefs. Well, we need to change your beliefs. The problem is that your mind does not want chaos, it wants everything in order and will do anything to get back to normal. The fact is we grow when there is some stress or unusual circumstances. Think about it, when you lift weights the only way that your muscle grows larger is through stressing it. Therefore, most people see stressful situations as a curse, but in fact, it could be a blessing in disguise. So the key is to look at these tough times that we go through as challenges to strengthen our character and grow.

Also, our belief about millionaires has to change. Most people have the mentality of keeping up with the Jones'. Everyone wants to give the appearance of being rich to prop up their egos and build their self-esteem but the ironic thing is that they are hurting themselves to become the person they are pretending to be.

With some small planning and rich "decisions," I truly believe that anyone can join that top 3%. Only a little over 2.5 % actually leave a million dollars or more behind. It is still amazing, and I bet you have done this: Was there ever a time when you wondered how do all those people live in those big houses or have those boats? Well, statistically it has been proven that only about 20% of those people who sail those boats are millionaires.

I was making over $200,000 a year since the age of 27, and I know that only about 3 percent of the population makes that kind of money. So how is it possible that all these people own these large ticket items? I love Brooks Brothers but only shop at the outlet stores because I have a hard time paying over $1,500 for a suit. Yet there are many of these expensive stores, and who are the people who get $100 haircuts and bottles of wine? Is it an inheritance perhaps? The statistics say otherwise, and in my business of meeting people with money, most came from middle to lower middle class backgrounds.

Perhaps it is their inner drive that makes them want to be millionaires? They value the dollar and are careful what they do with it and do not like debt. Most of the rich people buy $10 bottles of wine and do not drive a BMW. Mark this well: delayed gratification is one of the true keys to success. Spending all of your disposable income to have that home is not the way to go. This leaves less money to invest in businesses, investments, real estate or even yourself. Ninety percent of all millionaires live in homes valued at less than a million dollars, and many of the folks in those big homes do not really have adequate income to live there. Then of course if your neighbor has a pool then you need to have that too.

Let me ask you something. Why is it that 40% of physicians have a salary over $200,000 but only 10% are millionaires? The reason – consumption, the perception of success. (Could it be that they choose that profession for the same reason? Interestingly, most farmers have a higher net worth than most doctors.) If you truly think about it, it has to do with insecurity. You want that car so you can show people, "Hey, I am a success." Some say performance, quality of the car, etc. I say bullshit! If I took that emblem off that car and replaced it with a Chevy emblem, I bet the person who wanted to buy that Jaguar does not do so. Who wants to bet me that this is the truth?

As a matter of fact, most doctors and lawyers I have met have a small net worth compared to the small business owners at trade shows who own drycleaners, building companies, funeral parlors or garbage companies. You see, these people are rich not because they want all the toys but the driving force behind their success is financial independence and the freedom to do what they want with their time. Many do have these toys, but it is only after they have achieved their success.

Most millionaires do not become one until they are in their forties, which is why when I see a person driving that nice car in their 20s, I have to wonder that for most of them, was that the best place for their financial resources?

Here are a few more statistics provided by Thomas J Stanley, the author of the *Millionaire Next Door*, in his recent book *Stop Acting Rich*. First, out of 140 million income producing individuals in the United States, only 354,000 generated an income of $1 million or more. Most men have never spent more than $399 for their suit; only 7% own a bottle of wine that costs $100. In fact, most bought their wine between $10 and $25, and 90% own a car that cost less than $75,000.

There are so many misunderstandings and wrong perceptions about the wealthy. We think they are all concentrated in New York and California, yet most of the rich per population are located in the Midwest and South. 62% have never been divorced either. Is it that by having money there is one less thing to worry about? Less stress? The biggest stress that Americans have in the book *Stop Acting Rich* by Thomas J Stanley is the home that they buy. The home tends to dictate what we buy, and with Americans' mentality of keeping up with the "Joneses," we tend to spend money that we do not have. As a matter of fact, the average square footage of a home owned by a Chief Executive of a Standard and Poor's top 500 firm is only 5,600 square feet. (Judith Burns' "Sell Signal: When Boss Buys Trophy Home", *Wall Street Journal*, April 12, 2007, Page D6)

Most people listen to their accountants for advice, yet middle managers, business owners and engineers are the people you should be talking to because they are more likely to be millionaires than your accountant. Many did not come from money or even have parents who graduated college. Most came from families of blue collar workers. So hopefully that cleared up most of the preconceived notions of who the wealthy really are.

OK, now that we got that out of the way let's see how YOU can become one of those positive statistics. I am hoping that you bought this book for one of these reasons because listening to your friends will most likely not help you at all. Trust me, most of my closest friends have no money because they lack the mentality to reach past their comfort zones. The key then is to learn from people who have accomplished what you want to be or do.

First, I am writing this book under a pseudonym. I truly believe that we should share things that have produced good results in our own lives, things that can better people as a whole. However, I really do not want to "become famous" for writing self-help books, especially rehashing the same basic things through several different books. Also, I must have read over 100 books regarding the secret of becoming rich, and most of these say the same thing or mention just parts of what you really need to know to become rich. There are many books that are not full of substance or mention enough specifics to get you on your way to make you rich. They will tell you in a general sense but not be specific enough for you to get up and take action immediately. Let me give you a simple example. Let's say that you want a loaf of bread, many of these books will tell you that there are places that you can go to buy this loaf of bread and that there are many different kinds, but will stop short of really giving you all the information to actually get that loaf of bread right now. I will tell you where to go, the time the store is open, the price, the different kinds of breads, how each one will taste, and why you should have that particular loaf of bread so that you can leave that part of the book and do it immediately.

How am I able to do this? Because I have already done so. Let me tell you about myself very briefly. I am 45 years old. I am worth about $20 million. My father was a truck driver with a sixth grade education and my mother had just a high school diploma. We were lower middle class. I did not have a car, for example, until after I graduated college and was in the military. As a matter of fact, both sides of my family never had anyone graduate from college, I was the first. I was so naïve my first day in college that I thought they rang the bell to go to the next class. Was I a great student in high school? No, about a C average, and if I tell you what I received on my SATs you could try to guess what university would possibly accept such a low score. If it was not for a partial wrestling scholarship and a coach to give me a chance on a probationary status, college would not have been a possibility. Let me state right now that a college degree means nothing. I remember waiting for a job interview with about 30 possible candidates for the same position, and I was close enough to the door that I could actually hear the interview. These candidates were responding to the question, what did they learn from college? They would give these long responses such as "being a finance major I have learned how to react to market volatility, research companies, use the best methodology for evaluating companies, proper asset allocations, etc."

So when it came my turn to answer that question, I stated, "Nothing. It just taught me the ability to learn, and if you teach me I will learn and follow your instructions." Guess what? Right answer. I received the job because of that answer. The fact is that your high school teacher and college teacher did not know how to create wealth and become rich; if so the majority of them would not be teaching.

There is a famous quote by Calvin Coolidge that states "nothing in the world can take the place of persistence. Talent will not: nothing is more common than unsuccessful men with talent. Genius will not; unrewarded genius is almost a proverb. Education will not; the world is full of educated derelicts. Persistence and determination alone are omnipotent."

Now am I Donald Trump? No, but I do not think that many people can really relate to that kind of wealth, though I truly believe that anyone can have at least a 1-3 million dollars net worth. (Plus Mr. Trump had a little bit of a head start from his dad who already was a successful businessman, not to take anything away from what he accomplished since then which is impressive, but I came from nothing.) The bottom line is people are looking for happiness, not only in their professional lives but in marriage and health as well.

Furthermore, to become successful, others need to have faith in the things you are doing, making, or selling. They must see it as real worth. If they do then your success and prosperity is assured. Trust me when I say that the road to success has many detours and is always under construction, right now for me the road seems demolished, but I must push on and believe what I am writing you today because it is the truth even though doubt always rears its ugly head.

What I have done is break down the book into 5 specific sections.

A. Reconditioning the mind. Why are we going to spend so much time in this section? It is by far the most important section. A simple quote that I love from Gandhi is, "A man is but the product of his thoughts. What he thinks, he becomes." Success is truly a mental game. So, I will look in-depth at the spiritual side of how you act and think about wealth; your emotional state and the importance of visualization and meditation. You might say, "Why do I need to read this?" Please do not skip this section. Without this section you will not succeed because it takes a mentality and mindset to become rich. There are certain ways that you need to think about certain situations. Unlike most books that make comments about how you should be thinking, they do not give you exercises and methods to actually make changes. That's because they want you to attend one of their seminars or for them to coach you. Why? More revenue. You will have those weapons after you read this book. The greatest competition is with yourself and your subconscious mind will control you no matter how strong your will power.

B. Money / Investments. How do I know about this section? I am an extremely successful financial planner and speak to average folks on a day-to-day basis. I will finally speak to you the truth about investments and exactly what you should be doing.

C. Real Estate. I will sum up about 50 books just in this one section. This is a path to wealth that everyone can take and it should be a part of your roads to riches path. I will show you what banks are looking for, where to find the best deals, how to finance the properties, how to evaluate a property, and when to flip and when to hold.

D. Business owner. Let's face the facts. This is a key to wealth. Most people who come into my office who are rich are small business owners, and believe me, most of them are not the smartest apple in the bunch. They own drycleaners, pizza shops, Internet businesses, excavating companies, etc. Now if you work for someone right now, do not panic or think this section is not right for you. I will list many ways how to do things from your home a few hours a week and make money. Enough so that it is worth your time and possibly to perhaps quit your job to be your own boss. I can hear you now, "Yeah what a bunch of bull, I hear these promises all the time advertised on TV." Your mentality will change, and I will try to be so specific that you will be convinced of at least stating to yourself that this might actually work. The first section will help you overcome this mentality. This is why you are surprised when that C student whom you never thought would do anything with his/her life is now a millionaire.

E. Closing comments. The last thing you need to do and know.

The reason why we have sections on investments, real estate and business, is because to make your journey easier, if you just do the basics with each one of them, it will almost ensure your way of becoming a millionaire. If you just choose one path, you have to become an expert in that path to create the wealth that you need become a millionaire. For example, if you did not run your business that well, but did enough to quit your job (replace your income) you can have the time for real estate and investments. It has served its purpose because it frees up time, the greatest and most important asset you will ever have. Perhaps you have enough real estate properties to generate enough income to quit your job and concentrate on your own business, or have extra cash to invest, thus it has done its job for you to create wealth. By using all these sections and doing the basics I have just written in this book it almost makes it impossible for you not to succeed. I really would like to dumb you down, not think that much and just follow my instructions to the "t". If you would just do so, my promise to you is that I will make you rich.

The last thing that I would like to state before we get started is the reason why I am writing the book. This is my way of giving back. I truly believe and will talk about this to some extent in the book that all of us are rewarded by sharing our experience and knowledge to make this planet a better place to live for everyone. I thought about teaching people individually these secrets and comments, but I realized that I could make a greater contribution by writing a book and reaching thousands instead of trying to work one on one. So here are all my secrets, knowledge, experience, and wisdom of not only myself but also others who have taught me to become rich.

Part of learning something is reading and studying it. Wouldn't it be great if you could read any book on any subject just once and have it memorized or learned? So to truly get value out of this book, you need to read it more than once, highlight it, and memorize it. The least effective way of learning anything is by reading it and hearing lectures on a subject. The best way, the most effective way by far, is actually doing it.

The worst thing you can do in life is to never apply the things you learn. I love movies, and you can be the director of your own movie. Too many people let others decide how their life will turn out. Your mind is the director and the projector, let's make the end of the story a happy one. Let's get started.

First this book will be divided into four parts:

1. Mentality to become rich. DO NOT SKIP THIS SECTION. This is by far the most important aspect of becoming rich. I do not care if you think it is a bunch of bull. Your mind, whether it is athletics, finances, dealing with stress, etc. is by far the most important weapon you will ever have. The programming that is in your mind of your values, beliefs, assumptions, and truths, basically came from others, and it is very deep rooted or hard-wired in your subconscious. Most if it came from when you were younger than eight, so you had no chance since you were not in control of your life at that age. I will not only tell you how the rich think, what you need to think or feel, but show you how to reprogram your mind so that no matter what you are trying to do your odds of succeeding are greatly improved.

I am absolutely convinced that 75% of what is holding people back is inside them rather than their circumstances. The quality of your thinking determines the quality and reality of your life. The fact is when you raise your confidence and opinion of yourself and what you are capable of doing, then you will have the confidence to take more risk. Willpower will make you rise to whatever you believe you can achieve. It is really simple, and this is very powerful, and it all comes down to this: you can almost skip this section if you really get this and that is "you can choose what you pay attention to". (Do not skip this section, though since every part of our success is based off of our thoughts.)

2. The road to becoming rich and which paths to take. Believe it or not there are not many. I will tell you what paths there are and which ones anyone can take to create wealth. This will be a step-by-step guide in exactly what you need to do for the paths I will discuss. You should be able to take this book with you, do what is stated and create wealth by doing exactly what I tell you. Not in a general sense like most books that are available. They are full of philosophy but very short on substance. Success almost all of the time is small things done correctly consistently.

3. Finances. Since I am a financial advisor. The TRUTH will finally be told. I will tell you how to create wealth in this area. As I am writing this I actually cannot wait to get into this subject because once it is explained and, God willing, enough people read this section maybe it could make a difference in how people view their finances and finally know what to do. In this section, I will also show you how to save money today and what not to buy and to make sure you never get ripped off again.

4. Final comments. I will talk about truths of the universe and what every individual should be doing. Along with protecting your wealth that you created.

So basically, it will not be that difficult. First, get your mind in order. Second, choose the field in which you will begin to create wealth and take action immediately. Third, manage your finances along the way and after you create wealth, protecting your wealth since that is the responsibility of everyone who creates wealth. If it is not followed, the wealth will disappear. My only wish as I am about to begin is that someone would have told me these secrets when I was younger, but no matter what age you are as I write this book, it can be done, and my examples will prove this to be true. For many of us, we just think day to day or week to week, but the rich think year to year, and very rich decade to decade.

Part One: Mentality

THE NUMBER ONE obstacle in life is not money, talent, connections, your upbringing or surroundings. It is your mind. It is our biggest adversary. Without reprogramming, it is impossible to go over techniques on how to become wealthy. PERIOD! Three things in life motivate us: the desire for gain, the desire to be loved, and the fear of loss. Ask yourself why you would want to become rich? I have to believe that for most of us it is simply freedom - the ability to do what you want to do without worrying. It is for me. It is not to have a mentality of scarcity, like people have now in the recession that we are in, but an abundant mentality that there is more than enough money for everyone. That abundance mentality will make you seek that freedom mentality.

The whole goal of our lives is to live our lives fully, to become the best people we can and live up to our true potential. Unfortunately, will power alone, no matter how hard we try, will almost always end in defeat. You really have to change your subconscious. Why? It works 24-7. Think about it. You can put up bricks and work 12 hours a day, but if someone else is working 24 hours a day putting up bricks, it is almost impossible to beat them no matter how hard we work. So, the whole goal in life is to live a life full of purpose and to have few or no regrets upon death.

The key is to first master the art of thought. Why? Because your thoughts hold the key to every situation. Man makes himself what he wills. Wherever your attention is focused is what you become, you will know at the end of this book how to shift your attention to the results that you want. The way we do things is a direct result on how we think.

Therefore, the key is to train yourself on the way you want to think. I love the example by James Allen which references a garden. "If it is cultivated and tended to, it will flourish with a beautiful bounty of flowers and fruits, but if neglected and not attended to, weeds will fill the space and destroy the garden. So, we first need to get rid of the weeds".

Weeds are negative thoughts of hate, anger, jealousy, etc. It is actually quite simple. Good thoughts bear good fruit, bad thoughts bear bad fruit.

It is amazing that the outer conditions of a person's life can always be related to his inner state. The scary thing is once we realize we have control over our thoughts, we can become masters of ourselves and control our destiny and what makes us happy. So people really can control fate to some degree. To wish, will not help us, or to even pray will not help unless our thoughts and actions are harmonized with those prayer and wishes. I cannot think of anyone who does not wish for better things and finer circumstances, but nobody can have those things unless they are willing to improve themselves.

A person who is poor but unwilling to give his job his best effort, will deceive or even steal from his employer because he justifies in his mind that he is not getting paid enough. Or, he is too scared to get in "the game" and move away from his comfort zone and will continue to attract the same thing. Being poor is not just about money, family, circumstances or education. It is a state of mind. That is why we are spending a great deal of time on the "mind" section. Technically, that individual is expecting different results but continues to do the same thing. This is no different from the person who wants to lose weight and be healthy but continues to eat the same bad foods and always finds excuses not to exercise.

The problem in most cases is that unconsciously we are the cause of our circumstances. So in almost any circumstance, our suffering is the result of wrong thoughts. Therefore the big "realization" will come the day when we cease to complain, blame, or whine and search for the truth on how to change our lives. When we start to control our thoughts, we will find that the things that we want and the people we need will actually come to us. This transformation does not take long to occur, it can happen rather quickly. One of the greatest quotes I can share with you comes from James Allen, which states, "A man cannot directly choose his circumstances, but he can choose his thoughts, and so indirectly, yet surely, shape his circumstance."

So if you think back to the reference of the garden, when you plant hateful or selfish thoughts, the results will soon show up in your harvest. The same can be true of pure thoughts. Also when you raise your self image you will tolerate fewer judgmental comments about yourself and will not be as easily manipulated. Plus, you will learn patience. This is one of my weaknesses. You want what you want and you want it now. Patience is one of the keys to the wealthy, but a liability to the middle class. In the past I would buy things that

I thought would make my life better but all they did was take away my freedom. Discipline via delayed gratification is a key to wealth.

Health is also linked to thoughts. Happy marriages make us healthy, close family and friends' behavior can be contagious. Close relationships that have good habits behave the same way. It is a funny thing that the people who fear disease the most, through the power of the mind, are the most likely to get one. The reason is that by thinking of revenge, hate, envy, disappointment or other impure thoughts, it demoralizes the body which increases the susceptibility to disease.

The same is true when you are feeling good about life. It gives us the strength to eat the right foods and exercise, and we are optimistic about the future. The key to feeling this way is to live with a life of some purpose, so that your life has meaning. Because when times become tough, it is hard to live with conviction if you do not know the reason why you exist. Also, when you are not sure of your purpose in life, it is easy to fall into the feeling or become prey to impure thoughts of worrying, fear, self-pity, and hatred which are usually signs of weakness. Let's think about smoking cigarettes. There are not many people who for the first time picked up a cigarette and said, "Wow, that tastes great and makes me smell and feel good." So why do we smoke? Typically it is because of peer pressure from friends - wanting to fit in. In other words, we are willing to compromise our health in order to "be cool". So when you see people who smoke and cannot break the habit, it is a sign of weakness.

We might think that we should automatically know our purpose, but many times this is not the case for most of our life. So you can live with purpose immediately by focusing on something, even if it is a material possession. Whatever the key is, focus your attention on it, make it your duty and devote yourself to attaining it and do not allow yourself to wander away from this goal.

The true power of thought is through concentration, determination and self-control. So even if you fail there are always lessons gained. Perhaps it strengthened your character to prepare you for something greater. In order to obtain anything great in life sacrifice is typically needed. Sacrifice little you will gain little, sacrifice much and you will achieve much.

The same is true of gambling in Vegas. Think about it, the higher minimum bet amounts the more potential for gain. I always have much more respect for someone with little who has attained something great rather than someone who has a head start in life, typically if both are in the same position. This shows the person who started out with less has a stronger character.

In America, anyone who starts life with less means and is currently working hard labor and thinks of better things like grace and beauty, spends free time developing powers and talents will soon find his mind has become out of harmony with current circumstances. You can see this same individual years later in completely different circumstances. I am sure that many observing will state how lucky you have been without seeing the trials, struggles, disappointments and failures that you have endured.

There are fewer obstacles to success than people think or believe, not more. Most worry about what "could happen" but those things almost never actually occur. These made up possibilities paralyze most people from ever trying or continuing towards their path of reaching their goals.

The ironic thing is that people do not understand what risk really is. You need to understand something very deep, which is that seeking security is based upon fear. Fear is the killer of dreams. There is a big difference between survival and security and having abundance. Having security gives way to your freedom. Who has more freedom? The person working at the post office delivering your mail or the owner who owns three drycleaners run by a manager? Can the owner take off every Friday if he wants or take a month long vacation when he wants? The answer is yes, if it is run properly with the correct individual. Many think of having a steady job and paying off their mortgage as their ultimate goal, and the safest thing to do. Why is money important? The reason why is because it gives you freedom: freedom to buy what you want but more importantly, freedom to do what you want with your time.

Time is one of the most important things in your life. The true measure of wealth is time to do want you want to do. It is the ability to do what you want to do without worries of money issues. Think about it. If money was not an issue, what would you do? Pursue a different career, travel more, read or study more? Also, it does not make a difference how much money you make. I have a friend who makes over one million dollars a year but spends it all.

The key to having true wealth is what you keep or invest to create wealth because the fact is that if he could not work, he loses everything he has including a standard of living well below his current standards. The hardest lesson to learn is to create a lifestyle that needs less money than you are currently making so that you have money left over to create wealth.

The fact is if you ask people what their net worth is, I would bet that 90% could not give you an accurate number. The sad part is that people need to pay more attention to their net worth. Just by paying attention to it, it has to expand, just like with any thought. If you pay attention to a subject, either good or bad, it expands because your energy is focused there and the universe will assume this is what you want more of. So paying attention to your net worth is a good thing because this is one of the reasons I am sure you bought this book – to make your net worth grow.

One of the goals of reprogramming our minds is to develop the discipline of avoiding indulging in temporal rewards of luxury. To help in this endeavor, one simple exercise is necessary. I promise you that if you keep it where you can see it your odds of succeeding at anything go up 35%. Here it is and it is very simple: Make a list of areas in your life. Health, business, relationships, and dreams, such as traveling, accomplishing your black belt, or whatever it is. Write it down and list which goals are the most important – prioritize them. By the way, the biggest misconception is to choose goals that are not too lofty or grandiose. BULLCRAP! This is the biggest misconception. Dream big! We are limited only by our own thoughts, and this has been programmed into us and is simply not true. Things are not as tough as they appear.

Then create a little notebook with the goals listed in a prioritized manner. Keep the book where you can always see it. Next, the key is to break down a complex task into specific tasks. Let's say you want to open a restaurant. You have to make a business plan. The first step might be to look up on the Internet someone who can help or to get data that can tell you how to formalize a plan. Then break down what they are telling you into smaller steps. For me it was trying to conduct a seminar to get clients. First day's goal is to pick a location. Then pick a restaurant. Then find a marketing company for the mailing. Then do a mailing. Then find a topic on which to speak. Then study the speech one hour a day for three weeks. Then get the speech compliance approved. Then talk about the small details of the event, the food, the sign-up sheet, the attendees, etc. If you look at the task from a broad perspective, it will be intimidating. Breaking things down makes big tasks simple. Also, that does not mean to continue to do something that is not going to work, but rather it means to choose a different task to accomplish your goal. If you do not have a skill that is required, do not sweat it. We will talk about this later, there are many people who have the skill you need.

As individuals, we tend to put ourselves in small boxes. We limit ourselves to the potential we can possibly achieve. There are many forms of intelligence: emotional, interpersonal intelligence, logical intelligence, linguistic intelligence, etc. Some research suggests over 15 levels of areas to form an "Intelligent individual". Some are great speakers, some people can express their feelings to others, some people are great with numbers, some people can handle detailed physical tasks, some can "Read" or understand others; the list goes on. The point is that we all have strengths and abilities in some areas. To become successful, and to have an easy time of becoming successful, (and enjoying it the most) is this - do what you are good at and enjoy and delegate everything else if possible.

When people are educated on creating wealth they seek help from other sources outside themselves. A big reason why so many do so is because of a lack of education. In school they never taught us basic classes on investment or creating wealth. Instead, we study home economics or the War of 1812. Most of what we are taught has no real usefulness to help us in the "real world," and our teachers are even more uneducated on the basics of the subject of investments.

RESCUE ME… *A lot of people today are counting on the government to come in and save and protect them. This is not going to happen and these are people of desperation. Throwing money at the problem creates poverty. Many on disability or welfare have no motivation to improve their situation because they are afraid of losing their benefits. The biggest problem in America for example is the Medicaid system. It was not meant to be a long-term care provider. What is scary is that over half our population will need some type of long-term care, and only 1% has bought long term care insurance. We have to let go of the entitlement mentality. If you picked up this book to read you are not one of them, if you want to move to a higher level of living, then you have to leave behind your old level of thinking and adopt a new set of rules. Many people want to be told exactly what to do, so guess what is about to happen. These rules have been true but never taught to you.*

There is a shrinking middle class in the United States, so either you will be on the rich side or poor side. Other countries such as India and China are finally establishing a middle class and times are changing. I am worried about America because one thing that truly made us strong was the immigrant willing to do anything to make a better life. I see this sometimes in Mexican families where people will work three jobs and are happy for it. What happened to the Roman Empire was really the result of too much of the good life where people became complacent, thought they were too good to do menial tasks, and became lazy. They were unwilling to do what it took to become prosperous or sacrifice for their empire and the public welfare. In the past, did you know that India was the richest country on earth until the 17th century? India was also the oldest continuous civilization, as well as the largest. Today, India is the largest English-speaking nation in the world. Thirty eight percent of all doctors in the United States are Indian. (India also invented the number system and chess.) In which civilization would you rather have lived?

They say that the number one reason for our high divorce rate is money. There is a great saying that says you can give a man a fish or you can teach him how to fish and instead of feeding him for a day you can feed him for a lifetime.

Trust me, by becoming wealthy you can teach people to solve their own problems, and this is what God approves of and makes people truly happy. Many in the United States believe that they are entitled to benefits from the government, and when change has presented itself then people resist.

One of the reasons there was the mortgage crisis was because people could not afford the homes and banks were lending out too much money at a high loan to value ratio. It was not long ago that banks would only lend you 50% of what the house was worth. Think of when we tried to privatize social security. What an intense negative reaction! This has happened many times in the past. President Nixon tried to solve the trade deficit, so instead of our dollar being backed by gold it became just a fiat currency. This did not solve the real issue.

Here are some additional facts that I find interesting. The lowest fifth of the population earns $14,767, the second fifth earns $35,137, the third fifth earns $56,227, the fourth fifth earns $84,095 and the last fifth earns $176,292. 80% of the population earns less than $103,100 (as of 2012).

The reality is that Americans have become lazy and we as a society require instant gratification. We have turned into a nation of "we want it now" mentality. Also, please remember that there is evidence across religions that your God wants you to become wealthy. "Every blade of grass has its angels that bend over it and whisper, 'grow-grow!'" The Talmud also states, "May God give you of the dew of heaven, and the fatness of the earth, and plenty of grain and wine." Isaac in Genesis "There is nothing in the world more grievous than poverty." Midrash Exodus Rabbah 31:12. God wants you to ask for things. How about "And I say unto you, Ask, and it shall be given to you; For every one that asketh receiveth; and he that seeketh findeth; and to him that knocked it shall be opened." New Testament (Luke 11:9-10).

Reprogramming

The problems of our country are not going to disappear. We must learn to take care of ourselves. So throughout this book, I will teach you how to fish. Trust me, this is the only book you need to read. This is all self-help books combined into one. You should not just read this book, you need to highlight it, study it and learn it like it was part of a college or high school course to earn your degree. What you continuously practice and repeat something it becomes a habit. I compliment you on just reading this book. 80% of our population bought nonfiction books, and 9 out 10 people never finished the book they bought!

Wow, where do we begin? We are going to talk about some deep stuff. Things that will make your logical mind wonder if it is true or a bunch of bull**. I have a difficult task at hand. Most people, it is said, have core values and ways of doing things determined in their early teens. The only thing that changes people is a significant drastic emotional event. The reprogramming of the mind is so hard because, as stated earlier, most of it is hard wired in. Your conscious mind is the reasoning or rational part while the unconscious mind drives our actions and determines our habits.

You need to think of your unconscious as a warehouse unfortunately storing all your unlimited beliefs that you really do not want, continuously putting out negative waves that are taking you in directions you have no control of or want to go. Think about it - do you consciously want to let down your children, fight with your wife, disappoint your friends or boss? NO! The bottom line is that it is impossible to achieve long-term success unless you change your subconscious mind because your subconscious mind determines your long-term success. If every time you look in a mirror and keep saying that you cannot stand the way your body looks, then your wish is your subconscious' command to attract more of what you do not like. So we must have a shift in thought or consciousness when you realize what you are telling yourself, especially if it is what you do not want. The hard part is that you have to first appreciate the things you do like about your body then magically you will begin to take better care of yourself.

So, how do we change it? It could be changed through meditation, visualization and other techniques that we will discuss, but it is not something that can be fixed quickly, unless you have a way to erase memories and experiences. Moreover, your mind is very stubborn, meaning that even if the habit is not good for you and you consciously realize this, your mind will do everything in its power to make it true. Techniques, if followed repeatedly, will eventually create change. This is one of the goals of this book. For most though, coaching and therapy helps. With this out of the way, the actual techniques of creating wealth are rather easy.

It is kind of simple, we are part of nature. Everything is made up of light and energy. When you align yourself with the laws of nature life moves smoothly, when against it, life is tough. Everything is a result of our thoughts and actions. Your weight, the money you earn, your mind, your health: cause and effect. All right, everything is made of energy, this energy travels though vibration and frequency carried through the air.

When you make a declaration it carries a vibration. This vibration actually goes into the cells of your body. Ok, too deep, I will explain more. By the way, please keep an open mind. Nicolaus Copernicus, Giordano Bruno, and Galileo were either put to death or imprisoned for saying that the Earth revolved around the sun. It was not until about 1700 through Sir Isaac Newton that we took this fact to be true. First, everything that we are has to do not with our conscious mind but rather our subconscious.

When you say I am an A type personality or a driver, or a perfectionist, or whatever, it is because of your subconscious mind. So what you heard about money is ingrained in your mind from what you have been taught. Please do some research on lottery winners and you will see that most of them lose their winnings by poor decisions. You see, their minds and subconscious are not willing to accept the wealth, so even though they do not know it, their subconscious mind will not accept it. That is why people who lose weight put it back on six months, or one year later. The reason why they lose the money is because subconsciously they are trying to get rid of something else such as anger, so they replace it with something else instead of getting rid of the real problem, i.e. the anger. And trust me on this statement; money will not make you happy.

By sending out a declaration, the universe sends back a message to your subconscious mind. You cannot have two thoughts that contradict each other. You can visualize making a couple of hundred thousands of dollars a year, but then you sit down thirty minutes later and worry about how to pay the bills.

So here is the secret - you need to have your THOUGHTS and FEELINGS in order then take ACTION and you could have anything that your mind believes. You will never have a thought that is not achievable. This is why it is critical to be exactly sure of what you want - the more details the better. However, they all have to be put together. Also when you act, you need to act as though you are there - not where you are. Your past experiences and results in life were nothing more than your past thoughts. Also, getting upset about your past is counterproductive and does nothing to further your cause.

Even though you are not aware of it, the FIRST rule of changing your behavior is saying declarations even though you might not believe them to the universe, again - even though at this time you might not believe it. Sometimes you might not believe in something, but there is a thing called faith. At this point, this is what you have to have right now. I will tell you exactly what declarations you have to say later on. You see, first you think of something, that thought leads to an emotion, then the actions you take on that feeling leads to some result.

So first you have to recondition the mind. How do you do this? The first thing you have learned so far is declarations, even though you will feel silly and will be more of a chore for you and you will not believe why you are doing this. It is stated that thoughts create a molecular change and that by repetition you can change the neural pathways in your brain. When you keep saying that you have abundance, eventually the subconscious takes root in the mind and you become abundant.

An EXERCISE that you want to practice is to consciously keep track of your thoughts for one week and when negativity creeps into your mind, you must consciously change your pattern of thought. Through practice you will get much better at this, so in the beginning you should have this written down on your goal sheet when you awake and read right before you go to sleep. You first have to understand that you have been taught your thoughts by others and have to change those thoughts, which takes some reconditioning.

Of course, if you expect to recondition your mind overnight, you will be very disappointed. You have lifelong thoughts that have been programmed in your mind. Poor people think short term, they look for immediate gratification, and when it does not occur immediately, they give up. Envy can be a very damaging thought. Solomon in the Bible stated that envy is a more destructive emotion then even anger. Always try to remember the things that you are grateful for. The ironic part is starting with the hard things first, then throughout the rest of your life, it becomes easy.

Many times in this book I will repeat myself. I do so because sometimes things are quite simple, and I want you to really understand the concept that repetition is truly necessary so that an important point is emphasized. Through repetition you understand a point. Sometimes our frame of mind is important when finding the truth or finally learning a point. You can be trying to read with the TV on, or people talking in the background so an important point will be overlooked. Please remember that your thoughts of lack or "I am short of funds" puts a limit on your own consciousness. The fear of lack is only limited in the mind of man.

Faith is needed, to do activities with the faith that all things needful are provided and good will come. Pause before you begin your day and pray if necessary. For some a good prayer might be that, "Jehovah is my Shepherd, I shall not want." If you know how to take charge of the universal substance and mold it to your use then you will be prosperous. (Pretty deep, huh?) The key is to train the mind to become conscious of your thoughts.

I know people who are continuously focused that evil exists; but remember, evil conditions are not recognized by the divine mind. The affirmation that everything that comes into my life is good, and that I am only to have the good, will help your consciousness accepting and attracting what is good. I really do not know why this is the truth, but it is. Try it for yourself and you will be satisfied. The key is to continuously do this until it becomes a habit. Remember that everything that comes into your life is for a reason to bring you closer towards your goal. You have control over what you attract by simply what you think.

In these laws of the universe, you have to first be able to show that you can handle the blessing that you have already received. If you show that you can do this, you will be rewarded with more. You also have to be grateful for what you have regardless if it is not much. Do not focus on what you do not have or what is missing, but be grateful for some of the things you have right now like friends, family, health, etc. When you show gratitude and appreciation, the universe wants to give you more and people want to give you better service and you will get more attention from friends and family. It is true, try it with your spouse tonight.

For some people being grateful for their current circumstances will take some effort, but it is a rule that must be followed. I have had the opportunity to travel to India and after you see countries such as this, every American should be considered wealthy. Three billion people around the world live on less than $2 a day. It is all relevant. The reason for thinking positive and being grateful is that it builds positive energy, thus you will attract more of the same. The key is to focus on where you are going not where you have been. There could have been mistakes that you have made in the past, but there is nothing that you can do to change the past, it is a lesson learned that you must not repeat in the future. Stop focusing on lack. Look back at the past experience and be grateful for it, you might say there is no way I can do that – do you realize what happened to me? Well you can be grateful that you will never do that again or put yourself in that situation again. This is a huge handicap for most people. Focusing on unpleasant memories of the past only brings up things that you do not want and turns your attention to it. That is why it is so important to be around things and people you want to become or make you feel abundant. Please always remember that the energy will flow to where your thoughts are.

In a way we all need to become actors to some extent. Even though your current circumstances or current appearance might not warrant you to act boldly, you must do so anyway and sooner than you think it will be warranted. Please also remember that people will not treat you any better than how you treat yourself. You cannot look for others to provide you the comfort of trying to make you feel better, you must heal yourself first. You need to love yourself first.

I have read in several books to write 'thank you' on the bottom of your check to all the bills you pay, and the universe will reward you. Also, continuously ask for more of what you want. Believe it or not there is a correct way of asking for things. Ask for what you want, not for what you don't want. "Please God do not make me poor," is not the way to ask but rather, "Please God give me wealth and prosperity" is the right way.

We mentioned about faking it. The whole goal is to act when you do not see the light at the end of the tunnel. It takes sacrifice today in order to have the results that you want tomorrow. The whole key to first recognize true change is to really take responsibility for yourself. Being the victim is an easy choice. When you start taking responsibility and hold yourself accountable for things that happen to you, you then can be responsible for the changes you need to make. It is powerful knowing that you have the ability to control your destiny and no person or circumstances can affect you.

Visualization

If you raise your energy people become attracted to you. Why is this the case? Because energy can be transmitted through the air. Just like the sound of music can shake a chandelier. The subconscious mind is so strong that it is like the thermometer at your house. Your home could be a little cooler or hotter but eventually it will set itself to the correct temperature because that is what it is programmed to do. So if your mind is set to $50,000 a year, then that is what you will earn. If you set your sights on being comfortable, it is too vague of a concept for your mind to understand. It has to be very specific. Also you need to set your sights on becoming rich because if you miss your mark you could wind up being comfortable. You will look past opportunities that will enable you to make more but seek opportunities that could earn you the amount of money you are programmed to. The middle class has a tendency to believe that you have to have a lot of money to truly become successful. However, it is the right idea that will attract you to money. Try to avoid sharing your idea with people who have a limited mentality. Another way to talk about your subconscious is past conditioning or old habits.

We are creatures who have rituals, or more appropriately, habits that play a strong part regarding how our lives turn out. So there must be ways that we can recondition the mind to behave in a manner that move us towards our goals and the person we want to be. A way to recondition the mind is through visualization. Athletes do it all the time so that when the time arrives to perform they are used to the scenario presenting itself. It is much easier to do anything if you are used to it or have done it before and your body does not know the difference between what is real or imagined. Have you ever awakened from a nightmare, of when you were falling, in a cold sweat with your heart racing? Was it real? Of course not, but your body reacted to it like it was real. Your mind does not know fact from fiction. When you have thoughts that are satisfying to your subconscious, your mind will always want that encore performance. The key here is to have that encore performance in the real world so you can produce results. Not just results in your finances but in other areas such as relationships. I kept on getting into relationships with the same type of individual and reacting in the same inappropriate way. It was not until I understood more about the mind that I could break that pattern of behavior.

Can you imagine if you could program your mind that you love to wake up at 5:00 a.m. or a set time to do things that will bring you closer to your goals; how effective would your life be? But it takes repeated patterns of visualizing this concept, not just visualizing it a few times. When you begin to visualize, you need to think about the end result then look in the past through visualization of the steps you took to achieve that goal. The key is to again repeat the process and have a scheduled time to visualize just like you do with other tasks that need to be completed so that you can be relaxed during the process. Try to hold that picture in your mind and go through the details and the real emotions you will feel when you are accomplishing or have accomplished your goal. A great idea is to write down everything you would feel if you accomplished that goal. Read it before you visualize, then you can go over the details when you begin the process of visualization.

Details are very, very important: how you feel, how your family will feel, what it would look like, sound like, what it actually feels like, the colors, the time of day, etc. You visualize so that you can overcome your fears and self-doubt. Also, through your reticular activating system you will become aware of things that will help you achieve your goals. It will give you the strength to persist when times get tough. The ideal time to visualize is in the morning or at night. So you have to first be aware of your behavior and you cannot do this on your own. You need help from others that are close to you.

Ok, so one exercise that you must do is to ask people close to you about some of your behaviors and write them down. Take your emotions out of it and do not get hurt when people tell you what they think or if you disagree with them. Remember that this was your past you and how they perceived you, if you sincerely tell them that you are doing this to better yourself, most people will volunteer. This is a tough exercise and takes courage because, I do not know about you, but I hate it when people tell me things I do not like and I disagree with some of their beliefs about me, and I want to justify myself to them. Please stay away from this tendency; they will change their opinion about you once they start to see your results.

The first person you want to do this exercise with is with yourself. Write down all of your self beliefs such as "Some people are born lucky," or "I do not have the education or connections, to do that," or "Politicians are corrupt and have their own self-interest at hand," "Fat runs in my family" etc. This will reveal conflicts in your life where you need to grow. As I write this, I am going through some difficult times with my family. However, if we embrace the good times as well as the bad, I am hoping that I can learn and grow from the situation.

The bad times really dictate who we are if we do not have a positive mind. Anyone can be positive when things are going well, but it is your thought pattern when things or times are tough that shows if you are really on track to a positive attitude. To keep positive you must read positive books, visualize positive outcomes, pray and say your affirmations through repeated daily exercises. Through exercise we can change some of these beliefs that do not serve you so that you can choose a life that you really want to live. There are obviously emotions and past circumstances that had a deep effect on our lives, and to get past those issues, they need to be addressed. But for many of us, we let people control our emotions over trivial things. The real key is to be in control of your own emotions. No one really makes you mad, you do it to yourself. When you continue to be mad, you are really allowing that individual to control your life. You need to choose your emotions.

A great example for myself was I recently locked myself out of my home and asked my wife to come home at a certain hour to let me in the house. My wife, let's say, has a tendency to be late. Well, she was supposed to be home at 2:00 p.m. to let me in but showed up at 6:00 p.m. In the past, this would have ruined my day, and I would have let her have it when she arrived. Instead, I took a different approach. I took that time as an opportunity to work and do tasks outside my home and accomplished a great deal. Also, when she arrived, I was calm and polite. That evening we had a great time as a family. We have a choice of how we react to things that happen to us. Mastering your thoughts will eventually create vibrations that you want and will eventually attract what you want into your life.

To visualize, you need to bring up feelings or emotions that are positive. These emotions will eventually lead to actions and we know that actions will lead to results. A trick that I have learned by reading books on the subject is to create a vision board of the objects that you desire such as boats, cars, houses, the way you want your body to look, your family to be, etc.

Also do not just limit your board to material things but perhaps scholarships that you would like to be recognized for such as giving away a college scholarship in your name, or how you would like to be recognized by the press or community. Then sit quietly for 10-15 minutes and envision that you already have those items and are enjoying them and put emotion behind it. Sooner or later, you will start to attract these items. Also, please try to visualize first in the morning then once at night, again this is when your mind is most receptive to change.

People need to change what they are committed to or dedicated to doing. If you are broke, overweight or smoke cigarettes, to some degree you are dedicated to becoming so. Change your focus or commitment and you will change your results. You can never be happy if you focus on what you do not have, because your focus will always be on what you lack. When you focus on lack you try to find shortcuts, take unnecessary chances and try to rush for success.

The opposite is true when you focus on too much of what you have, especially if you had some great success. This turns into arrogance and mistakes happen easily when we think we know or can do anything.

Also, feed your mind just like you feed your body. Stop buying fiction books and buy books that can enhance your progress and actually finish the book. TV – I do love TV, but please no negative movies before you sleep since it just replays in your subconscious all night. Also, the news really is all about negativity, be selective in what you choose to watch. It kills me when people say they do not have time. Can you imagine if just half the time you spent in a car was listening to learn a language or something that can actually enhance your life? You have to make a conscious decision that what you are doing is adding value, not taking value away.

So, pick up an audio book on owning a business, real estate, anything that will add value in your life. Pick up one book. And no TV after a certain time at night. If you do just this, watch what you can accomplish and feed your mind with. It will be amazing.

Most of our programming comes from the ages of 3- 8 years old so it takes work to reprogram our minds. What is hard to believe is that a thought, even if it does not serve you or is actually a detriment to your progress, will do everything in its power to make itself true at all times even when you do not want this to be the case. It is difficult to change and you need to do something in many cases that causes enough pain to finally make that change.

The good thing is that we can experience change by just using our imagination. Again, the mind does not distinguish between fiction and non-fiction. So using your imagination to feel that your desired outcome is actually coming true, and it is a positive feeling or reaction, your mind will want more of the same thing. Change your temperature gear in your mind, meaning in your house when it either gets too hot or too cold, the temperature gear will adjust the temperature higher or lower to keep the temperature as is. That is why when people get an unexpected inheritance or bonus something like their furnace breaks down for the same amount they received. Your unconscious mind runs 24 hours a day while your will power is limited.

You want your mind, unconscious, and conscious to work together. As I mentioned before, think of your unconscious mind as a warehouse that stores ALL of your decisions, limiting beliefs, emotions and experiences. Just like your muscles; when you put them under stress they will grow. Well, the molecules in your mind will grow stronger and change as well but only through repetition.

How do you get repetition without actually experiencing things? Well, as stated earlier, through visualization. Remember that the mind cannot distinguish what is real or unreal, so just like you exercise the body you must do the same thing for the mind as well.

It is this simple, be very clear on what you want, if it is a business, detail everything from the pictures, colors, furniture, etc. Then, visualize it in the morning and at night before you go to sleep. And make sure it is written down. Please keep in mind that it might be tough in the beginning just like you were sore when you first starting working out, but it will become easier over time.

Vibrations

Just like the Beach Boys singing about Good Vibrations, there's also bad vibrations that you can send out to the world. Be careful of how you judge things that are happening to you. Right now I am going through a difficult time with my family, but as I really look at my situation, I might not like it but it is a blessing because it is a lesson on what I need to change in my life.

A task that I have not quite mastered yet is my emotions. No one can make you angry but only yourself, and you give them power and control when you allow that individual to do that to you. The ultimate goal in life is to be able to choose your emotions rather than having people or circumstances control you. Controlling your emotions does not mean ignoring them. The key is to give yourself permission to recognize what you are feeling and to have empathy for yourself.

You will know that you are progressing when you look back at a situation or circumstance that just affected you and realize how you handled it compared to what you have done in the past. I remember that I would come home and the house would be a mess and it would leave me with a feeling of unsettlement. Then it would affect me the whole night. Now I just accept it and have an understanding that everything cannot be perfect and that my children and wife did not do this on purpose. I am able to relax and not have it affect my moods. Then I realize it was not as big a deal as I made it out to be. Please try to focus your emotions on the positive feelings that will let you have a healthier, less stressful and happier life; focus on love, enthusiasm and gratitude.

The key is having vibrations that attract what you want and you do this by choosing emotions that will bring the right vibrations. Good vibrations. Everything that comes into your life is what you want. I know this is tough, but if you really wanted to find something good about your situation, you can and, through time, will realize the blessings. An exercise to do right now is to write down a belief you want and develop the actions you need to have it in place for good.

One of the first rules that you need to follow is to stop blaming others for your problems. Also, negative thoughts such as anger and revenge are prohibitive for your growth. I would have to tell you that FEAR is one of the worst emotions that people can have (along with blame, worry, and guilt). Most fear is unwarranted because our minds are making assumptions that might never come true. Fear is also based on the absence of personal control over situations. Malcolm Forbes stated, "Keeping score of old scores and scars, getting even and one upping, always make you less then you are." By bringing up misfortunes in your past you are giving them energy to occur in the future. Also, if you were wronged, you are giving power back to that individual or circumstance to affect you in the present.

Justifying your behavior is the same as blaming others. Sayings such as "money does not buy happiness" will program your mind to believe that if you have money you will not be happy. So, of course, you want to be happy so your subconscious will not allow you to have a significant amount of money. That statement is ridiculous because money has nothing to do with happiness. Neither does the reaching of that goal or purchasing a toy create happiness, it is the attitude you have while getting or achieving these things. It is harmony in all parts of your life that will make you truly happy. Being severely unbalanced in any one area creates unhappiness. You can have a great relationship with your spouse but be broke, you can be rich but your relationship with your spouse, children and loved ones is not right. There are many people who are rich who are not happy just as there are many people who have money and are very happy. These sayings were made up by poor people to justify their situation.

What is truly amazing is that you can become what you want by changing your thoughts and your focus. So, one of the keys is to become aware of your feelings. When you find yourself complaining about something, you are creating negative energy, and you do not want to attract negative opportunities or energy but positive. So please steer clear of negative people or complainers because this energy they are projecting will be attracted to you. Just as when you see an inspirational movie or a sad one, do you not walk out of that movie with those emotions? It is like being around people who are sick. Eventually you will catch a cold. When people complain to others they want attention. We are influenced by the people with whom we keep company. Try an exercise and see if for just two days you can go without complaining once. You need to keep a notebook next to you to mark down when and if you complain. This exercise is very powerful and will be explained in more detail throughout this book.

I mentioned fear earlier. When you fear something, your mind focuses on the negativity such as "what if I fail?" or "it will never work." That keeps the mind from thinking of possibilities, or worse, stops you from trying before you even attempted to try. How are you going to have a reward unless you take some risk? In order for your mind to attract the things that you want, you have to be sending the same message. Just think if you told a child to eat healthy but only provided junk food to eat.

Another mentality to become aware of is the "I want it now" mentality. It is like wanting to have a muscular body now but have not having lifted any weights. First, you have to reprogram your mind and invest, then the rewards will show up. The problem is if you are not willing to pay the price for success. Can you work 12 hour plus days? Are you willing to give up your recreation or hobbies temporarily? It is like the person who wants to lose weight but cannot give up the fatty foods or exercise. How you know you are on the right path is when you are feeling some level of discomfort. Why, because in order to grow you have to reach past your area of comfort. You need to tell yourself that when you feel uncomfortable about something you are actually growing. It is like lifting weights or running. Perhaps you could only run a half a mile, but through repetition you can now run a mile. The half mile run is not as uncomfortable as it used to be, thus you have expanded your comfort zone and are a better person for it.

If you do not ever push yourself beyond your comfort zone, this is what will happen. First, you will never be happy. The key in life is to be the best person you can be in all areas of your life. The only way of challenging yourself is to reach past comfort zones. There are fewer obstacles than you imagine there are. People have a tendency to dwell on every objection or obstacle there is in any situation and thus they prevent themselves from that first real estate deal, business venture, or money making idea. Being comfortable is the killer of dreams.

Your body and mind will tell you when you are growing, and you can measure your growth by doing something when you really do not feel like doing the task. Once you complete your task, you can be assured that you have grown. It is truly amazing how many worries we have imagined about things that will never happen. Think about the times you have thought of negative outcomes that have never occurred. The most important thing in life that you can do to control your happiness is to control your mind. Control your thoughts and you ensure your success. The way to control your thoughts is to become consciously aware of how you are feeling. If it is a negative feeling then you are aware that this is an unwanted thought. With practice, you can control the way you think. This is very powerful, please do not read this and move on. Write it down where you can see it every day. This simple message is the key to happiness and success. Once you do make that commitment it is truly amazing how the universe will support you.

Please remember that the person you hold an image of is the person that you will become. The purpose of the mentality section is to encourage you to take action. Also, do not share your dreams with others who might not be supportive of you. If the people you hang around with do not share the qualities that you do or are small minded and do not have the character you inspire to be, then spend less time around them. I am not saying to dump them but spend less time with them. Find a mentor. Most people are flattered and will voluntarily give of their time. The key is to maintain a focus.

The rich have an almost continuous focus on what they want while the poor continuously focus on what they do not want. You have to be able to see opportunities, and you cannot see opportunities when you are not focused on them. You need to focus on making and investing monies - not spending it, at least in the beginning. If it is true that what you focus on expands, then this is a great place to start your focus. A great way to change your behavior is to focus on what you are grateful for. Is it no wonder that according to a Seligman study that optimists outperformed pessimists ten to one. Is anyone surprised at this outcome?

The key to getting more is to focus on what you currently have and are grateful for. But be warned, doing affirmations, visualizing what you want and meditating alone will not bring about what you want. Action is necessary. Most people will never take action though because they are afraid. Fear can paralyze you, and it is one of the biggest obstacles to success. You need to have courage. Courage is taking action even though you are afraid. In the beginning, you need to fake it even though you will be unsure of yourself, doubt yourself, or feel uncomfortable. It is not enough to visualize and do affirmations. You must act and speak like you really are receiving it because your brain does not know the difference. The key is to believe like you already have it today/now.

An important note is to think of positive things and as state before visualize before you go to sleep. When you were younger and watched that scary movie before you went to sleep that is all your mind focused on the whole night. So feed your subconscious with what you want to happen. Since your mind cannot distinguish between reality and what is not real, you need to make believe. The bottom line is that if you send out signals that you cannot have or afford the things you desire, you will send out signals to that effect and it will be so. Speak the opposite and watch what happens.

Also, it is important in the way you ask the question. Did you ever say, "I can't afford it?" We all have. Instead ask the question in the right frame which is "how can I afford it?" I remember when I graduated from graduate school and all I really had was one nice suit and shoes, a tie and a coat while walking in New York City. I felt like a millionaire, and a lady walked up to me and said,

"You must be one of the Wall Street types." Little did she know I did not have two pennies to rub together, but the feeling was great. So faking it will eventually bring what you want.

Albert Einstein said, "When I examine myself and my methods of thought, I come to the conclusion that the gift of fantasy has meant more to me than my talent for absorbing positive knowledge."

You need to pretend the future has arrived now to accelerate what you want. The past is just what it is: the past. But by focusing on it you are actually reliving the past, the key is to focus on the future and what you do want. By focusing on people who have hurt you or past circumstances, you are giving power back to those individuals or events. Do you want to give them that control? Now, it takes energy-action and knowledge but you will never explore what you want or have the courage if you do not change your mentality.

(This next section is not related to Mindset?)

Spend Wisely

I think that when people have wealth they waste it foolishly. There are many stories of celebrities who made millions of dollars a year and go bankrupt just a few years later. It is actually quite the opposite. The wealthy are very savvy spenders. Often, they do not pay the retail prices that most Americans do. You will see that they have the confidence to always ask for a discount. I say the word "confidence" because that is what it really is. When I go to a hotel I always ask for a free upgrade and many times receive it. In the past, my attitude would have been "who do you think you are to ask for an upgrade – the president?" The key is to ask or at least say, "Can you do any better?"

Some ideas to consider are to shop at large wholesale stores such as BJ's. I have a friend who bought a great home out of college and was making the same money I was, and I could barely afford the rent. What did he do? He bought the home but rented out the rooms in the house. Thus, he was paying less than what I was renting a one bedroom apartment for and he sold that home for a very nice profit a few years later when I just wasted my money on rent payments. Also by just threatening to refinance with another lender when rates dropped he even lowered his rate and thus lower his payments. (Always ask for a discount.)

Another easy way to live the lifestyle you want now, and it is made even easier with the Internet, is to house sit. People, rich people, have houses that they do not have a chance to visit as often as they want and need people to check up on them or house sit. This could be a great way to stay in a beautiful vacation home for free. We have always been told buy used, not new cars, because they lose so much value as soon as the car is driven off the lot. Look in the papers or befriend a wholesaler and pay him a fee for when he finds the car that you want. If you are a safe driver, think about raising the deductible. Look at raising the deductible on your house and your health insurance as well. Also please shop around. I am amazed at the number of people who do not get more than one quote. Your goal should be at least three quotes. Now there are areas you should not skimp on for the purpose of success. You need to look the part. If you are dressed for success it will make you feel and act more successfully and people always tend to respond to people who look sharp.

Go to a consignment shop if you have to or change shirts and ties with the same suit. One of the things you want to get in the habit of doing is to ask when the next sale is. The sales clerk will tell you. Then look at buying the item you want.

Wealthy individuals do not eat fast food. When they do eat out, rather than what you would think, they eat at fine restaurants. I do not care if you can only afford the salad and a glass of water. Eat there. Why? Because there are connections there. Also you become who you associate with.

On a side note, wherever you do eat, watch the company that you are with. If your friends are overweight and they are all eating dessert, trust me you will do the same compared to people who are conscious of what they eat.

Love to travel? This is truly one of my passions! Become a travel agent. My wife became an agent by simply joining an organization and filling out some forms. Now we get great discounts, upgrades and free trips to difficult locations just by sharing the website with her friends and our family. Many times we put together group trips, and because of the number of people who attend, we get to go for free. Also, as stated earlier, always ask for an upgrade. I actually saw this in a movie starring Cameron Diaz, and I tried it and it works. You can swap houses. I swapped houses with a person in Ireland who actually owned a small castle for three weeks. It was great, better than staying at a hotel, and without the cost. (I swapped my vacation home in Utah which needed to be looked at and I had not been there in over a year).

Another great thing to do to help get rid of debt or find some needed cash is to have a garage sale. It's a wonderful way to clean out your home and make some money as well. Also it can be a great way to give to charity.

We talked about visualization, but sometimes it is very difficult to do when you are just looking at a picture. So visit your dream home or go to the dealership and drive your dream car. This will make it almost a reality and can speed up the process of getting what you want.

So remember that you are the only person who can plant your thoughts. Thoughts have a ripple effect. Think about it. The images that you put in your mind form the image of who you are. The more intense your thoughts the more likely the outcome, so try to think of good thoughts, catch yourself when negative sayings or thoughts come to mind. Remember there is no shortage of anything except in what we believe. Opportunities will come your way if you embrace this attitude of unlimited abundance. In the good book it says, "He which soweth sparingly shall reap also sparingly; and he which soweth bountifully shall reap also bountifully." II Corinthians 9:6.

So let's recap. Tell yourself a new story of how you want your life to be. (It has seemed that in my life I have had extremes of highs and lows in not only my career but my marriage. This is a tough way to live, and I believe the goal should be to try to live a more steady balance.) You do this is by thinking about how you want things to be. There is a vibrational switch to the things you want to attract. If you speak it often you will start feeling what you are telling yourself. Simply put, your words and thoughts are the reason you are who you are. Negative things like fear, anger, and jealousy are emotions outside of what you want to become or the person you are capable of becoming. So repeated negative thoughts, just like an illness in your body, will over time prove to be true to some degree.

The secret to almost all success is to keep yourself happy. If you think about it, that is all everyone really wants in life. People who change jobs or change relationships often are always trying to find something/someone that will make them happy. What they are taking into the relationship though is themselves. So that is why no mate or new job will bring satisfaction. It might work temporarily, but it always comes back to yourself. Appreciation is the golden key to attracting what you want. Also by simply just asking God, they say that the wealth of the universe will come to you. (Too deep, huh – or what a bunch of bullshit?) Some tips are to write things down, not that you want it but that you already have it. Do not ask for money, because that is not specific. A nice home, a loving relationship, a happy family or a nice car, these are things that are specific. If you really do not know what you want, then you will get nothing; ask for nothing, you get nothing.

Please remember that the power of thought is more powerful than we can understand or imagine. When you become inspired, then act on it immediately, it did not just come randomly to you.

Something that people can understand is the rule of cause and effect. Talking bad about someone else comes back to hurt you. This one is actually tough for me, as I am always a person who thinks about justice and that it has been my job to get it. As I was thinking those thoughts, I really did not know it was coming back to hurt me. I had to consciously forgive myself when I thought of bad thoughts about someone. Try to allow only good thoughts to come into your mind or come out of your mouth, and soon you will harvest those good things. So sometimes in life it is not as difficult as we think it really is.

Make up a list, visualize what you want, and get enthusiastic about it — that will help get what you want. You do not have to make up the list more than once, once is enough. Also do not tell anyone, this should be personal between you and your god, not for everyone to view. The only time to share is if it involves another person such as your spouse for a home or vacation.

The key to that list of the things you want is in the details. If it is a new car, what color, does it have Sirius/XM radio, are the seats leather or cloth? A good idea that costs you nothing is to visit the car dealership that has the car you desire, the Yacht Club that has that boat or read magazines that have those homes. Try to feel like it is already yours. The key to having what YOU want is to remember it is what you want.

Trying to control another person's behavior or decide what is best for them is not possible, and believe me, I have tried this with my wife. Also, once you write them down there is no reason to dwell on them, because by doing so means you have no faith. God will sometime provide a way that we cannot understand. God stated to "ask and ye shall receive." By trying to do it yourself shows a lack of faith. Also do not continue to write things down that you want, always ask for new things. By stopping to ask, you stop receiving.

I have mentioned that being happy now regardless of your situation is very important. So you must not care if you get it or not, be happy with your current situation and believe it or not, by not caring if you get it or not will help speed up the process. Acting in faith does not mean doing nothing, continue to work and look for opportunities. When they arrive, listen to your heart and take action. Lastly, a great exercise that is very important is to give your mind a command before you are about to go to sleep. Your unconscious mind usually remembers your last thoughts and works on those thoughts all night. Furthermore, I always keep a pad next to my bed because the universe likes speed and you could have a great idea, not take action, and that thought passes to someone who is ready to take action on his/her thoughts.

So everything that you do either adds to your success, takes away from it or adds no value. The key is to become conscious of everything you do. Do you watch junk TV, or mindless radio shows or listen to CDs that can help you and expand your mind and bring you closer to your goals? Get organized. Being unorganized and sloppy is what is reflected from the inside of us. So, one exercise is this: Clean your home, throw away everything you really do not need, fix everything broken, and you will get a renewed focus on the things that really matter. Trust me, this exercise should be THE FIRST thing everyone should do. It creates immediate results and gives us a sense of power that we are organizing our lives so that we can move forward. Then focus on the outer world of a haircut or new clothes.

We should know by now that we attract things through the vibrations we send out. How we raise these vibrations is by constantly immersing ourselves in things that make us happy, giving us confidence and strength and avoiding anything that is negative. As your thoughts change so will your life and what you want in life. It just takes a shift in your conscious mind then doing the exercise to shift the unconscious mind so that it works 24 hours a day without effort. Be especially careful of the negative words that you say to yourself.

Remember to take time for yourself and be happy. Life is truly not all work and no play. Being happy will make you more prosperous. Why? Because if you remember what I stated in the previous pages, your appreciation level and thoughts are what are important to getting more of what you want. So the happier you are, the more prosperous you will be because it is more of what you are attracting. An idea I have heard of before that actually works is to wear a rubber band and slap it against your wrist when negative thoughts or statements come to you.

Remember to control your thinking which will then control your behavior to get the outcomes that you desire. Be careful of the words you choose, especially if they do not serve your purpose because they can come back to you. The purpose of your wealth is to serve others. When you create jobs, you employ others, if you pass your wisdom to others, you will help them create wealth for others. Also, each one of us possess strengths. The key is to be aware of the strengths that we possess and use them. Lastly, remember that to have true success is to have freedom from money, time to do what you want, relationship success, and success in health and spiritual success. .

So now that you've heard all of this stuff, you still might be thinking that is still a bunch of bull. But let me ask you something: what if it isn't, and I am right? If you ask yourself that question, and if I am right, then it would be worse for you not to have read anything in this book because before you had the excuse of ignorance, now you do not. So, give it a try and fake it for a while.

No matter how successful I become, I always have self-doubt in my mind that states, "Who are you kidding, what makes you think you could write a book?" It tells me that I am not living up to my potential. Do I have to keep on giving examples? Believe in yourself. Ignore the people who doubt you, for they cannot follow you because they are filled with negativity and are not open to the truth. With blind faith, follow these instructions and the doubt of whether it is true or not will soon be revealed.

There will be tough times where you question yourself - that everything you have learned is wrong. The key is to continue to do the things written in these pages when self-doubt rolls in. You must change first before you have the prosperity that you want.

When you start to change, it seems that these are the darkest times. I do not know if it is evil that presents itself because we are about to change for the benefit of the universe; the key to remember is that God will not abandon you, and He is rearranging your life to make room for better times. So when things get really bad, things look really dark, you need to trust that success is on its way, and whatever is happening to you will pass. The ONE key is not to give up on yourself - the system you have learned. Keep in mind that bad times, stormy weather, and bad luck are indications that wealth and growth are coming your way.

Faith is the act of acting without knowing the future, believing that you will benefit from what you are sowing. If things get tough, write a letter to God explaining your situation and thank Him in advance for helping you – faith. Also if you want to be rich, think of rich things! Sounds simple, but in order to be rich you need to give the signal that you want rich things, such as $150 shoes instead of $65 dollar shoes, valet park your car at a fine restaurant instead of parking it yourself. Material things do not really matter, but what they do is help us learn our lessons of faith and a belief in ourselves. The book of Proverbs are there for true wisdom. Proverbs 2:12-17 states, "Wine and Luxury are not the way to riches."

When you ask for something, life might give you a lesson you are not ready for. Have a belief that what you receive is exactly the lesson you need at that point in time. Many have laughed at times when they have won over odds that seemed impossible. That is what makes the journey fun.

Can you imagine that everything you asked for came to you without effort? It would be unrewarding and not fulfilling. The fun is not the end itself but the journey to the end result. With deep faith, fear or being afraid will disappear because trusting in God or the universe is powerful beyond our belief. With this belief you will not have to save and then buy, you will buy then expect the money to come.

If you would have told me 15 years ago what I am about to say I would say that it was "hippy stuff" from the sixties, and I never liked that era (I would have fit in better in the forties and fifties). Try to think well of everyone and bless people you would hate. If you yelled at someone on the highway, like I have done many times in the past, remember that it comes back to you ten times stronger. So, I think of the consequences today before I make those statements.

The only way you will ever truly fail in life is to give up and stop trying. Love the life you have, stay happy and enthusiastic, and as a book I read awhile back states, "Don't sweat the small stuff." Trust that success is waiting for you. The strength of this mindset expressed above will help you when rejection comes your way and you fail in your endeavors. Your state of mind will attract things to you but you have to be able to see the opportunities and the courage to believe that you can do them, especially when everything is against you: money, education, connections, health, age, race, ability, time, etc. This mindset will give you the courage to do the things you are afraid of. Your mind will bring you what you are looking for. So many people ask the question, "how can I make an extra $20,000" instead of "how can I create one million." Creating $20,000 might be getting a second job or saving an extra couple of hundred dollars, but when you think a million, you think a business, writing a book, buying real estate, etc. That gut instinct sometimes comes from the unknown, but unfortunately most people ignore it.

So let's talk about things that we need to implement in our lives, just like brushing our teeth. I will call them DAILY PRACTICES:

1. Say your affirmations daily. As stated before, do them as if they already exist. The second part is to ask questions – Why? What you say out loud has twice the effect of saying things silently to yourself. The more senses you use, like emotion, verbalization, and visualization the speedier the process of them sinking into your subconscious. You can even get your spouse involved to tell you what you want to become. One thing that I used to do with my employees was use negative reinforcement. For example, I would say "You are always late," but by saying this I was getting more of what I did not want from my employees. It was when I used different words that I actually noticed that things started to improve and that is when I really noticed that "hey, maybe these things really work."

2. Write down your goals on index cards or laminate them on paper. Make sure you carry them with you to work and read them twice a day. You can even ask questions and then flip the card over for the answer. Say them first thing in the morning then as the last thing before you go to bed. This is when your mind is the most open to ideas, and it will help you keep focused on what you need to accomplish that day to reach closer to your goal. Then at night your mind will come up with solutions to help you get to where you need to be. Your mind will work for you without effort. Writing down your goals is one step

up and more effective than just saying them because it involves more effort. You can see it, and you use more senses. Again, try to write at night before you go to sleep and wake up in the morning because your brain waves slow down, and you are more receptive to receiving ideas and having them sink into your subconscious.

3. Stay away from the local news and newspapers that have negative news. Be selective in what you listen to and read. Also, if friends say things about you that are negative such as, "you know that you are impatient," correct them and say you used to be that way and ask them to support you in your transformation. If they are unwilling, it might be worth staying away from them.

4. Visualization. The key to this exercise is to visualize like you already have it and then remember the steps you took to get there. And most importantly, use emotions. That is why I think that pictures are so important. We are visual creatures and our minds think in pictures. Try it right now. Think of a chair, and your mind automatically visualizes a chair. You cannot say something without visualizing it. So put what you want on a board, I use a cork board, some people use a book. It does not make a difference, and I have pictures of everything I want from the body I would like to have to the boats and cars. Sometimes when I visualize, I use motivating music that inspires me. When you visualize, think that you already possess these qualities or items. If you can actually drive that car or go through that model home, or try on that watch, then even better. Imagine that you actually own it now. It will help raise your energy and keep you motivated on the prize. Professional athletes and Olympians do it, and your mind does not know the difference. Think about if you had a bad dream and your heart was racing or you woke up sweating. Not only visualize goals but visualize vacations and virtually anything you want in your life.

5. Feed your mind by reading books, self-help, or autobiographies on people who did what you are trying to accomplish. Listen to their struggles and see what their feelings were and notice how they kept persevering.

6. Time. We have to be more conscious of it. Try getting up just one hour earlier every day. Sleep is like a drug, and sucks up a lot of the most precious commodity we have which is time. What you spend your time

doing is an indication of what you value. The old saying of how you eat an elephant, "one bite at a time," is the way time can be used for us. Just one hour extra a day is seven hours a week or an extra 364 hours a year. Boy, what can you accomplish with all this extra time?

7. Have a technique at night that relaxes you. Meditate, listen to calming music, pray, say your affirmations, or read inspirational, motivating material. Also, write out your to-do list the night before and when you have thoughts that are important, and get it off your mind by writing it down. I always keep a pad and pen next to my bed. This also means taking two vacations a year within six months of each other. Also try to relax and not be needy trying to chase success. Do not be like the dog that chases the rabbit around the track but never catches it. It is just the law of attraction. It is the science of the universe.

HEALTH AND DIET

EXERCISE – 1. First you need to find out what you really want in life for:

A. Your health
B. Your relationship with your spouse and children
C. Your wealth
D. Your Spiritual health.

There should not be any questions as to why a balance in all areas is important. Because without one are you truly wealthy? You could have a billion dollars but not be able to walk down a flight of steps, have a great relationship but be broke, etc. Also, all of us tend to be strong in one area but weak in another. So the first exercise is to stop reading and focus on what you really want in each of these areas and then write them out.

I cannot stress this area enough, your outer body, which gives you mental strength and energy reflects to the world who you are. The sad fact is that 64% of Americans over the age of 20 are overweight which contributes to wrinkles and sagging skin, causes stress, aging, and high cholesterol which leads to heart disease. Lifting weights is just as important as running and cardio. Muscle burns calories, and aerobic exercise strengthens the heart.

Diet. (by the way – why we spent so much time on the mentality section is because close to 80% of all illness can be associated with psychological stress.) Here is something deep that I am about to state. Stuffing ourselves with bad foods, and you know what they are, is a way to avoid something that is bothering us and a way of avoiding our true feelings - a short-term solution to how we are feeling. One of the ways to combat this is to pay attention to who you spend your time with, meaning that if your friends order that cheesecake and are overweight, chances are you will be influenced and will be the same. Remember the law of attraction, we went over this already. Lastly, the reason why it is very important that we spent so much time on the mentality section is because your mental image of yourself, or any negativity that surrounds you, is evident in your physical appearance.

So steaks and white bread, pasta, rice, and potatoes take a lot of work to digest, and they make you tired because it takes a lot of energy to digest while vegetables and fruits take less energy. We need all the energy we can, especially if you are going to change and finally reach your goals. Be careful with not only what you eat but what you drink as well, such as soda. The acidity kills enzymes and studies have shown that a can a day can actually increase your chances of a heart attack.

Here is the simplest diet I can give you: eat just vegetables, fruits, fish, and meat. Stay away from everything else. I know I said that meat is hard to digest but the vegetables will help digest the meat. Just keep way from bread, pizza (which I love), and pasta. Eat small meals throughout the day instead of stuffing yourself. Also, exercise. Why does everyone have to be told that this is important? It increases bone density, releases stress, is great for your heart and skin, gives you more energy, makes us happier by releasing chemicals to the brain, increases our self-esteem, makes you look better, etc. Also, there has to be a combination of lifting weights which will reduce your acidity, and will help raise your metabolism. Then you can run or use that elliptical machine and please do not forget to stretch.

Also, there has to be some intensity to your workout which will actually give you a benefit. If you can read that magazine and exercise at the same time then that is a sign that intensity is lacking.

What I truly believe is that genetics has something to do with cancer but what we eat as well. The good foods are usually the bad as well, such as bacon, ice cream, macaroni, mayonnaise, white rice, and of course fried foods while foods such as bananas, oranges, apples, watermelon, nuts, cucumbers, green beans, lettuce, garlic, and asparagus can help reduce the acidity in the body which is a cause of cancer and helps supply more oxygen. There are ways of finding out what the acidity is with a PH test found in health food stores. Also, please drink plenty of water since it helps clean out the toxins in your body.

Moreover, take it easy on the coffee, since that too will help bring your levels of acidity up.

Additionally, many of us have heard that red, not white wine, have health benefits. A study of the French and Italians proves this. Do not forget the natural and great taste of honey, a great alternative to the sweets that you might crave. Everyone wants to make diets complicated, so here it is in a quick summary. I truly believe that everyone should read a book on the right foods that can help with whatever illness you may have because many can be helped by just changing your diet.

Pay It Forward

The hardest thing to understand is for many people who are trying to create wealth is that you do not need things to make you happy and the obsession of getting things will only push you further away from achieving them.

It is like John F. Kennedy stated but I will say it in another way. Give your full attention to serving people - the world and you will have everything you need. Inventing the light bulb, the computer, the telephone, Facebook are all examples of serving people that in turn served the world. If you concentrate on this, people will give you the money that you need and, in turn, make you rich.

In my business, helping as many people as I can in finances and help achieve their goals will ultimately make me rich - not trying to get as much commissions or fees as I can.

By serving, as I stated with the heavy stuff in previous pages, you will attract everything you need and more. Give without expectation. If it is having a video arcade then give people what they want and show them attractions that are new and unique to give them the pleasure they are seeking, not a game that stinks and brings in the revenue you want. If your area is working for a ski area or race track, provide it in a way that you are giving people what they need and want. The fact is you will be happier breaking free of the constraints of toys and the accumulation of just money.

Dont't Worry, Be Happy

The key is to be happy with your current situation or the status in your current life and your obstacles will eventually disappear. You are in a temporary situation and hope for the future will get you to where you want to be. Trust me, because once you get what you want, it will not make you happy because we are put on this earth with only one object, the ability to always want to grow. If you are worried about losing things, it can prevent you from growth. If I was worried about losing my job as a mortgage broker making over $200,000 a year, it would have prevented me from becoming an advisor where I made $8,000,000 a year. Too many people make this mistake.

First, make sure that what you are doing is really a belief in your heart. Even though I was making good money as a mortgage broker, I was not happy that I was selling 14% mortgages to consolidate credit card bills. Next, give the world what it wants without worry about getting paid. OK, I can hear you know saying – WHAT? I love the movie The Social Network because that is exactly what they did when they gave their program to universities without worrying where the money was coming from. Look to solve problems for people and you will become rich. Keep focused on giving.

At your work, if you do give, you will get noticed. If you start a business – give. Give and you will be a magnet to draw in what you want. It is going to take hard work, but hard work with a selfish mean attitude will not help your cause. Giving and attraction is huge. The key when you give is not to worry that you are getting nothing in return. God will take what you are giving and reward you for your gifts. Do not worry about a response or being awarded immediately. It will come.

The key sometimes is to be in a position willing to listen for it — and to work hard and have faith.

Meditation and Prayer

Meditation is so important because you have to be willing to hear the idea when it comes instead of having your mind cluttered. It will clear your mind. Meditation will help you relax and prevent you from wasting energy on things that you cannot control. In the military you have to be cool under pressure, especially when making critical decisions. Meditation will help you do so when stress enters your life.

Strive so that no matter how stressful or dire the situation may look, you are able to operate in a calm, positive, clear-focused mind. This is what will make you successful and accelerate your performance. To make your life easier, you MUST operate from a clear, focused, happy mind.

Unfortunately, people close to me have used prescription drugs to help them find peace. Yet, this does not work in the long run. Have you ever had a time when you were working and time stood still? Meditation could have that effect on your concentration.

As an advisor, I get turned down all the time. I struggled with this aspect and would get angry when I felt I was disrespected. The key would be to be happy when getting rejected as well. If I could not distinguish between the two, then I would have more energy instead of it being drained and would have the will to continue to call.

Happiness is contagious, and as we learned earlier, could be passed on to others. I have been right many times, but when I would put someone down or made my point very clear, in a mean spirited way, I was never able to close a deal or convince them to change or switch. I was always much more influential when I was able to speak with excitement and a happy way of approaching a meeting. I still have a tendency that if people are disagreeing with me to make it a personal battle, and perhaps I learned this in my wrestling days when aggression would give me the results I was looking for.

In business dealings though, it is much more effective to come out of a testy situation with a gracious presence because no matter how angry I became, it never changed the results. The key was to keep contacting people who could help without worrying about whether I was going to get paid for my efforts and trust that someone would listen to the help that I was trying to provide. When I sold mortgages, other salesmen would get frustrated with me because I was not tracking my "numbers." I was not worried about the results, instead I continued to focus on my work and doing the job rights and because of that, I was always the top producer for the entire company.

In summary:

1. *Constantly immerse yourself in things that give you pleasure and power and avoid experiences or things that weaken you. Love is the most powerful force in the universe. Feeling love and enthusiasm creates a vibrating positive field around you that attracts other positive things. Keep your mind on love and what you really have to remember is that what you think about yourself is right. If you think something is too large for you to handle, then you do not obviously have good thoughts about that subject, so that is what you will receive. Time, long or short, is not relevant or conceivable to the law of attraction.*

2. *Organize your life, the universe likes order, so first clear out old junk and get organized. Replace anything broken and work on projects that have to be done that you neglected in the past. You want the impression that you are in control, not what you have been in the past. You want everything to reflect where you are going, not where you have been.*

3. *Make a list of what you want in the physical realm as well as spiritual and your social world. Please remember that you were born to be great but have been held back by programming of mediocrity. Never forget that true wealth is balance in all areas of your life, not just extreme excess in one area.*

Religion in Relation to Prosperity

It is said that there is a substance in which all things are made that fills the universe. It is also known that God wants you to have everything you want.

Many of these great teachers wanted us to be like them, to mirror their behavior. We all have God within us. It was Jesus who said in (John 10:34) "God standeth in the congregation of the mighty; he judges among the gods." Also in (Psalms 82:1-6), "Ye are gods; and all of you are the children of the most high." God wants prosperity because it is he who enjoys and appreciates happiness. In Ecclesiastes 10:19 it is stated, "A feast is made for laughter, and wine maketh merry: but money answereth all things." Some people will say that self-sacrifice and poverty are pleasing to God. Jesus said, "I come that you might have life and that you might have it more abundantly." Is it a sin to be poor? I agree with Bernard Shaw who stated, "Lack of money is the root of all evil." Also, I believe it is a sin if all you love is money and use resources and people to get what you want. So if you get wealthy by helping others, I hope that you are the richest man on the planet. Is our life better by using the telephone, computer, car, etc.? I believe God wants us to have as much as we want for ourselves as long as we do good by others and handle our success with humility. God does not want suffering so how could this be true? If this is true then it is our job to focus and express God's desires.

One of the keys as stated earlier is gratitude. We all have received gifts. The gift of just seeing is a gift. So when you are not grateful for what you have – you are breaking ties with God. It is the same when we give gifts to someone and they truly appreciate that gift, it makes us want to give more. So a BIG key is to be grateful continuously, Jesus was continuously grateful saying thank you to God many of times in the Bible. Always give thanks. To lose momentum and lose ground is to be dissatisfied. Religion can be closely tied to your values, meaning that if you have a negative value to wealth you created or your parents created, you will sabotage your success.

God truly wants all of us to have wealth, there are so many references in the Bible to how to "think right" to get what you want. Mathew 21:22, "And in all things. Whatsoever ye shall ask in prayer, believing, ye shall receive and ye shall have." Let's give some examples. Jesus said, "Whosoever shall not doubt in his heart, but shall believe what he said cometh to pass, he shall have it." Faith is all over the Bible. Have faith and turn your thinking into prosperity and you will have it regardless what men around you are thinking. Have faith and the source will always surely give.

People will always confuse scriptures; wars have started over interpretations. When Jesus said that that it is hard for a rich man to enter heaven, it does not mean that it is hard because of his wealth because a poor man will not get in any easier or faster. It was meant to mean a person's thoughts on wealth - whether it controls them, whether they worship money, how they use their wealth that keeps men out of the kingdom.

With any religion, the key is to be aware of the presence of a living substance, the more it will manifest itself to you and will make you richer if it is only for the common good. Think about this, if you truly believed in God, then you would have no fear and worries, and faith will truly change your finances.

In Matthew 6:25-27, Jesus said, "That is why I tell you not to worry about everyday life – whether you have enough food and drink, or enough clothes to wear. Isn't life more than food, and your body more than clothing? Look at the birds. They don't plant and harvest or store food in barns, for your heavenly Father feeds them. And aren't you far more valuable to Him than they are? Can all your worries add a single moment to your life?" Also if you truly believed in God you would know that He would never put a desire into you that could not be fulfilled.

We have discussed meditation, but prayer is related to that. Your mind is like a muscle that with exercise becomes stronger. The whole key here is to invest more of your time on the thoughts you want instead of the outcomes and thoughts you do not want. In the Bible, Elijah had to practice through prayer and affirmation many times before he demonstrated the rain. Patience, something I lacked in the past, is the key.

What is faith? It is the ability to act like you are already receiving, praise what you have, and affirm abundance so that through your consciousness it appears. Zacharias doubted having a son because of the age of his wife, thus it had a difficult time manifesting. Jesus had an ability that I truly believe that we all possess inside us and can learn to develop to produce miracles ourselves, it is contact through faith. It is simple. We are accountable by our smallest words and you think in an appreciative way and abundance will come your way. Nobody needs to be poor, and it is a sin to be poor. Jesus' example of this the prodigal son. In this he was discussing the sin of lack, but by many it was used to preach about the moral sinner. In the Bible it is stated to "bring forth the best robe and put it on him." He even put a gold ring on the prodigal son which is evidence of prosperity. We must interpret it as is.

Jesus also expressed that "a youth wasted his substance in a far country where the divine law of plenty was not realized." Man shall have what he wants, what he earns through his efforts and abilities and laziness is discouraged. We get what we want and work for. Too many people talk and think that things will come to them with no action. Without action, anything will cease to act.

The fact is that God loves us and wants the best for us, so when we are caught in the act of, "I haven't enough to pay the bills" do a quick affirmation of prosperity. Become disciplined in your affirmations, then eventually it will sink into your subconscious when you are awake or asleep. This is why I am a big believer in saying affirmations right before you asleep. Make your last thoughts be on prosperity. Try to banish all thoughts of being a slave to poverty. Also, God will reward us as we evolve with our possessions as we have the ability to handle them. So the key is to affirm, meditate, then accept the gifts. Think of the many movie stars or athletes who after they receive the gift cannot accept them and subconsciously destroy what they have been given. So be prepared to be alert and accept the gift when it comes.

A deep thought is to remember that faith is never in the light but in the dark, meaning that if we could see what will become of our faith then there would be no reason for faith. Unfortunately, this is not possible, so faith is necessary. You also need to be clear of what you want. If you are not specific then how does the universe know what to give you? Think about that! It would be like your spouse wanting something but never expressing in any way what he/she really wants. So know what you want and want it badly enough so that it is in your thoughts often. Have faith that the thing you want is already yours. God will see that you are thinking things that have not happened yet, and if you truly believe that, it will be given to you in real faith. Does this mean praying every day for it – no – God just needs to hear it once. Jesus said, "Use not vain repetitions as the heathen do, for your father knoweth that ye have need of these things before ye ask him." Soon things will happen and the laziness of the mind and love of ease will dissipate to get the things you want. Whatever you can imagine yourself doing I really believe that you can do.

When you pray, the best thing you can pray for is not riches or material possessions but wisdom. King Solomon asked for wisdom then developed it himself. I am guilty of dwelling on things that have been negative in my life, but by doing so you prolong your stay and make your progress slower. Visualizing and concentration is good but without faith, failure will come. Say your affirmation when you pray, because begging when you pray is not a prayer of faith but doubt. See yourself already having because God wants you to have it now. When doubts come in, do not entertain them. The Lord does not mean for you to sit down and do nothing. Why do the already rich get richer? That is not fair! That is because their idea of plenty is so interwoven into their subconscious that it is a part of them. They have a prosperity consciousness.

There is a sin to wealth. That is hoarding it and not allowing it to freely circulate throughout the world to those who need it. The fact is that in the Bible talks about three stewards given money. Two of them came back with more while the other was afraid to lose any money so never invested it and came back with the same amount given. He was then cursed for doing so. (Mathew 25: 14-30) Those who contribute wealth to the masses are a salvation to their country. Many countries throughout the world are examples of hoarding outlandish wealth for themselves and keeping their masses in poverty. You cannot limit the thought of wealth alone, it is the first step but you must become competent plus cheerful to fulfill the second law. The mind is so powerful. A great quote from Charles Fillmore stated that, "No disease, poverty, or any other negative condition can enter into our domain unless we invite it. Nor can it remain with us unless we entertain it." Hard to believe but the mind is that powerful.

The key is to eliminate all negative thoughts that come into our mind. Some of us have created negative thoughts from our past "hard times." The key is to eliminate such thoughts because all they can do is contribute the reality to us. Deny that you can lose anything and form the habit of blessing everything that you have. When we bless what we have, we are complying with a divine law that will continue to bless us even more. The biggest emotion that you will have to overcome is fear. Fear breeds poverty, it breaks down positive thoughts and produces negative ones that in turn bring in negative conditions.

As stated before, sometimes we must fake it at first. Never make negative comments in your home, even though it may be true, if you do not want to have this negative situation to exist. In a spiritual sense, by talking poverty and lack you are having them in your home as welcomed guests.

Thus, talk and think about God's substance and plenty that you would like to exist and then your unwelcomed guest of lack and poverty will leave. Also, never condemn those who have more. Do not think that they accumulated their wealth because they were dishonest in how they received their money. It is really none of your business. Your object is to get what is yours.

Love is the key to God's riches and thoughts of worry keep good from you. Also, do not try to will other people in order to get them to do what you desire. The only person you need to will is yourself. Remember that God does not reward the unbeliever. If this is the case, then guard your thoughts. Do not think of poverty or concern yourself with it, focus on the future and better times. Surrounding yourself with poverty does not help. Surrounding yourself with poverty gives you thoughts of poverty.

To most, the 6:00 p.m. newscast is the wrongdoings and tragedy of others that makes the headlines. These thoughts can stay with us for long periods of time. Your goal is to help the poor and needy and to fill their minds with hope and wealth. The poor and downtrodden need hope and inspiration to rise out of their circumstances. What will a free meal do, it will help temporarily but will remind them of their circumstances. There is nothing more inspiring to the poor than seeing a person in their same circumstances, or better yet, in worse circumstances, who has climbed out of their despair and has risen above their circumstances. You too should, at least for the time being, forget your tough past and stop telling stories of hardships so that you can dwell upon better things. Your mind can only focus on one thing at a time, so leave it for thoughts of what you want. Once you achieve wealth for yourself, then the goal is to spread the truth and break people from their ignorance of not knowing the truth that there is wealth for them too.

Try to carry each step in your imagination like it was actually occurring. Do not try to keep the knowledge to yourself. In the 23rd chapter of Mathew, Jesus pointed out the lust of the Pharisees to be called "Masters" to sit in high places and dominate others and take advantage of the less fortunate. What you want for yourself you should want for others.

Another example is in the Old Testament in the 4th chapter of II Kings. Read it, the two children represent the thoughts of debt. Jehovah always promised riches to anyone who listened to His commandments. As anyone should know when it comes to religion, forgiveness is typically preached. In order to allow the spirit in, you must be able to forgive. If you think about it logically, how can you allow in good, if your mind is full of hatred. If our God was to keep track of our behavior we would all be in trouble, but God is a forgiving God and erases those thoughts. We need to behave the same with negative thoughts of worry and fear. Debt always disappears when we have wisdom and good thoughts in control. Selfishness is a good way to increase your debt.

The real objective of what God wants is not wealth, or becoming famous, but developing our character to become the best person we can be. My intentions of this book are not for everyone to become filthy rich, but to provide characteristics that are fundamental to prosperity. The key is to understand that there is an omnipresent substance from which all things come and by the action of our mind try to connect with that substance to fulfill our needs and desires. PLEASE understand that what we have been talking about does not mean personal action. Action will move the forces in your environment to move towards you. The key is to take it day by day.

The smallest things that you do not do that should be done can have an effect on your life that you cannot imagine. I remember one day I had on my to do list to drop off a document that was 25 minutes out of my way and could have been done the next day. It was on my to do list and I wanted to show my faith and discipline to accomplish the tasks as stated on my list. Well, as I dropped off a document, I had a conversation with a person that led to a business partnership that made, and continues to make, me hundreds of thousands of dollars a year.

I want to emphasize that this book is not meant to be on religion, nor am I the greatest person at quoting scriptures. Many people will think that just following the rules of the Bible makes them more spiritual than others. However if your heart is not into the rules, following it does not make a difference what your actions are. The purpose of this section is to understand that there is a higher power that can give you the strength to succeed and knowing that there is this force behind you is very powerful and will give you that extra edge to push yourself when rejection and self-doubt will creep in. The truth is we always have a distorted vision of who we really are. Only God can give us the strength and put things in our life that will help clear that vision. The key here is that, whatever is troubling you, learn how to pass that burden on to someone else who can help alleviate the stress.

OK, those are some heavy thoughts and many people will laugh today over such deep "bull crap" as some would say. But guess what? They did the same things back in the day in the Bible. The Philistines laughed at the idea that words can overcome conditions. Trusting in the universe and faith in the goodness of a higher power for your wellbeing is essential. It enables you to look at things that happen in your life that are not beneficial as happening for a reason that will help you become happier and more successful. If you can look at the beneficial aspect of a setback, it will enable you to keep trying and persistence is one of the most important traits you can have. Do not ever forget that God wants you to be happy.

We think of heaven as a joyful place and God has stated, "Thy kingdom come on earth as it is in heaven." There are going to be bad things that happen in your life, and there will be many tests, but the key to remember is that the Creator of the universe wants what is best for you. It is essential to use the talents that God gave you. Trust in God that He will show you the keys to wealth, the gold, the end of the rainbow. In Proverbs, which is great when it comes to wisdom, (3;5-6 , 9-10) states, "Trust in the Lord with all thine heart, and lean not unto thine own understanding. In all thy ways acknowledge Him, and He shall direct thy paths. Honor the Lord with thy substance, and with the first fruits of all thine increase: So shall thy barns be filled with plenty, and thy presses shall burst out with new wine."

Trust me when I say that God wants you to become successful. Well, how the hell do you know this? Just think about it. We become tempted and vulnerable to sin when we are not happy with our lives. Why do people steal or murder or do any other crime for that matter? If people were truly content, there would be no crime.

Per capita, which countries have the worst crime rates? Do I really need to mention which countries they are? What theme is common in all these countries? Poverty. Absolutely! All that any man wishes for is to be loved and have a spiritual connection with God.

One of the greatest books ever written when it comes to wealth is *The Richest Man in Babylon*. It talks about laws of money that still hold true today as they did many years ago. If you read the book, it talks about the importance of having a recurring revenue stream. To have other sources of income that do not require you to earn it to make it. (Ex: Other businesses or passive income like investments or real estate.) It also states about saving 10% of what you make and the effects of compounding interest. Also, it says that you must seek advice from those who are competent to give it and to be aware of the promises of "get rich quick schemes."

The book does not say to save everything that you possibly can. Too many people I see as an advisor come in with these grand ideas of saving too much per month that is really not sustainable. *The Richest Man in Babylon* warns of this, stating, "do not overstrain or try to save too much." I agree, it brings too much discouragement and can sacrifice your way of living which can make you bitter or even more discouraged.

Just like in the past, the book also says that are spending increases along with our income. The book further states that it does not always matter what you make but how much you keep or what you do with your earnings to make it work for you or grow. In addition, it mentions character traits such as mastering procrastination, carrying your friends' burdens, working with people who have a successful track record already, and protecting your assets. I think the most impressive thing about the book is that it is a law that any man could use to create true wealth, and you do not have to be of royal blood to do so.

These are rules that applied 8,000 years ago and remain applicable today. Throughout history, we've had a tendency to repeat the same mistakes and in most situations we can learn from individuals who already made the mistake and have written it down for us to learn from. These principles in this book are not difficult to learn and anyone can implement them. I think what we have learned since then is that we did not know how to reprogram the mind so that we can implement these teachings. Changing our behavior so that we can follow these rules is the first step to making permanent change.

Moreover, here is something that I find comfort in. If you believe in a higher power, and right now you are experiencing something negative, then you know that it is merely part of a larger plan to teach you lessons to make you a better person and have personal growth. So to have a right minded way of thinking is to accept challenges as a gift to help us grow. Your thoughts and how you feel are the keys to attracting what you want.

Controlling Your Emotions

Boy, if you think about it, this is the key to everything. A lot of violence comes about by not being able to control or contain our personal stress. In most situations, we get really upset by things that are occurring to us and seem so important, only to see months and years later that what happened was a blessing. They really did not deserve the importance we put on them at the time. The only control you will always have in your life is the ability to control your thoughts and reactions to things that occur around you or happen to you.

By changing the way you think, you can change what you attract to yourself, which means do not concentrate on what you do not want. Think like a successful person, and you will soon become one. You become what you think about most of the time.

Always think about what you want and how to get it. Learn to be an optimist until it becomes a habit or a conditioned response to circumstances that happen to you. Once it is programmed into your mind, you will have more energy, need less sleep, be happier, and your immune system will get stronger.

To become an optimist, you must focus on what you want to have in the future. Envision yourself having it already and soon you will have it because your mind will seek out ways to get it. This reminds me of the adult elephant who will stay in the spot of the small rope that holds him because he thinks of the past when he was young when that rope was able to hold him still. Then it is as simple as making a list, a deadline, the steps needed and then just "do it" as Nike would say. Not trying to do everything at once but just taking an action every day gets you closer to that goal.

You also want to feel that by yourself getting rich, you are making others rich as well. It is said that when you find a person who is boastful that deep down they are afraid and full of doubt. Have quiet reassurance that you are becoming rich and are already rich. Remember that words are not always the most important thing to have people attracted to you. When your thoughts are right, others will be attracted to you by your presence. People will follow those from whom they can benefit, so take pride in knowing that you are increasing people's wealth.

Dictators, poor or Third World countries lack vision and leadership. It was the leaders who ruled for their own self-gratification. What is great about bad behavior that can impede your progress is just recognizing that you are feeling these thoughts. So, when you feel guilt, have hidden secrets, need to blame people, criticize others, and feel shame, this should be a signal to redirect how you are feeling.

Also, please understand that we are only human, and some of the greatest men in history had many weaknesses. Just look at our past presidents. You have just read the spiritual chapter, and here is one last example: King David committed adultery and then had his lover's husband killed. A murderer, David lied and tried to cover up the murder. Wow – that is some bad stuff. The key is to seek growth and God will never abandon that request. It is only when we give up that all hope is lost. We will all be tested by difficult people – even Jesus had Judas.

Every person we meet has the capacity to energize us or take that energy away. The key is to be able to master your emotions or at least be able to recognize the people who drain our energy. Having the ability to recognize that you cannot control people through your own efforts is a great strength to have. Only through prayer could you have the ability to create change in others.

What is the dark side of life? It is the negative thoughts on your mind such as revenge, anger, fear, resenting things in the past, distrust, and envy. The key to avoiding these behaviors is to remember that everything comes back to you and you do not want these attitudes coming back to you. So try to be conscious to project positive thoughts, thoughts of love. Regarding drugs: Sometimes they are necessary, however, when we take drugs they can help but they will never get to the underlying problem so that it can be resolved. The problem is people do not use drugs as a temporary solution but rather a permanent one.

Accept personal responsibility instead of continuously blaming others. If we do not take responsibility but instead project our own shortcomings onto others, we ignore our weaknesses and never address them so that we can become the person that we are hoping to be. I am guilty of this behavior. Why is this important? It creates negative emotions when you criticize or blame. You keep your focus on "what ifs" instead of focusing on moving forward. Too many people dwell on the negativity which slows them for looking for a solution. When you accept personal responsibility, it gives you a sense of control over your life that will then give you confidence and capability. Blaming others allows you to give control to others, and when other people have control over you, you have less empowerment and become a victim of your circumstances.

The real key to having control of how we feel is awareness. It is stopping for a second, which took a lot of practice for me, and saying what am I feeling at this moment, and recognizing how you are feeling. Then recognize something positive that can come out of the situation and have less emphasis towards your current feelings. Sometimes talking to yourself helps. I remember getting let go from a broker / dealer for no significant reason - getting fired, and reminding myself that I had been in this situation before and still succeeded.

Be careful not to expect perfection. The fact is you are going to sometimes feel angry, frustrated, it is how you deal with your emotions. This is important after you intentionally recognize these feelings, recognize your feelings, and ask God to remove them.

Also, too many of us hold on to way too much baggage that instead of occupying our minds on the future and what is ahead of us, we continue to relive our past. I used to do this with people with whom I was angry and every time there were circumstances, places, people, I would see that I would relive what happened and continue to think of revenge. What I have found is to recognize my hurt feelings but then to consciously choose to overlook the past situation.

There are some basic emotions that all of us should avoid, and they are anger, pride, impulsive reactions, envy, hate, lack, and poverty. Also, we have a tendency to overreact, and things are never really as bad as we think.

Boy, I struggled with this. I am the type of person who can cry watching a movie and be singing a few minutes later when a happy song comes on. Some people would say that medicine would help but the truth of understanding your emotions is the true way of controlling them.

ANGER, this was a big one for me because most of my early success early in life came from aggressive sports such as football and wrestling where letting your emotions go or anger could actually be useful. But in most areas, anger is a terrible emotion to let run rampant. Unfortunately, a true statement that most great leaders have found out in history is that it is better to be respected and feared than to be loved. Whether you own a business, or are captain of an athletic team, or head of your household, there are times when you must make tough decisions. If you try to please everyone because of your fear of being disliked, people will take advantage of your kindness. To make people better, you sometimes have to push them to do things they do not want to do.

Even in the Bible, we get the example of Moses who took people from a complacent state to struggle in the desert for 40 years. I am sure there were many who despised him and wanted to even kill him, but with his strong leadership and the help of some miracles, he eventually led his people to a better life.

Being soft will make people not work as hard as their potential can lead them to be and then, when you decide to get tough, people will take it personally because your behavior has changed towards them. Through your fearless attitude you will gain respect, and as long as you produce the results, people will bear with your approach because they will respect you. You cannot consistently have this attitude without times of really genuinely rewarding people, but it will be much better than trying to be nice to everyone because of the fear of not being liked. Strong fearless leadership requires you to set goals so that people can visualize the results. They look to the leader to see the strength to believe, so you must be fearless, strongly believe that what you are doing is right, and get excited that it is the right direction. Then find those who have close to your qualities and promote them to carry out instructions to the team. There is GOOD ANGER it is primarily for awareness, for self-defense especially back in the past when we were getting chased around by dinosaurs.

Anger intensifies situations, sometimes just the tone of our voice makes matters better. How do we behave in an argument? By taking control of our words and focusing on achieving a realistic outcome for both parties - not trying to win, like I have done almost my whole life, trying to prove that I was right. Every male has one underlying need. That is to be RESPECTED. While a woman's basic needs are to be valued and secure. Harsh and destructive language, we know what they are, the ones that push buttons of people you are close to never really provide the outcome that you want. The tone of your voice and kind, gentle words always make the outcome more successful.

One of the keys is thinking about words before you actually say them, which is difficult to do in an argument. If we could somehow have a vision of the future of the consequences of the conflict, I am sure we would behave differently. We typically come down to the level of our attackers, and attacking the argument is better than attacking the person, which we all know so well that we do. Ways that we can help with the conflict is to try to not prolong it by continuing to use harsh words. It is like putting more wood on a bonfire. Be quick to forgive. Perhaps send a small gift.

I learned the hard way that anger can destroy a marriage because it has caused a divorce in my own life and it is the most destructive force in a relationship. I would have temper tantrums and then feel bad afterwards and try to rationalize it after the fight was over, and try to resume the relationship. In the Bible it states that "he who is slow to anger has great understanding, but he who is quick-tempered exacts folly." When you are irrational, your vision is blurred and you do not see the reality of your actions. Being able to control your anger not only helps with your personal life but at the workplace as well. It brings more respect from others. Being respected by men is the deep root of the cause of anger especially when our expectations are not met.

When my spouse did not live up to my expectations, I took it that she did not value or appreciate me. I used her to meet my happiness and fulfillment. I was not truly able to manage my anger until I started to reflect on what I was about to say. I have always had the thought in my head before the person was finished talking, it was not until I actually paused before I made my comment that I was able to start to repair my relationships.

History's largest importance is to try not to repeat foolish behavior. Anger was the main cause of my home not being a safe haven for myself or my family. I was part of the problem. Why this is important is because you must have some type of environment where you can recharge your batteries. Instead, there was verbal abuse, tense moments, and a place for discouragement. Until I realized that I was part of the problem, the outcome was predictable. A great quote that I love from Benjamin Franklin is, "Any fool can criticize, condemn, and complain and most fools do."

Stay away from people who complain or criticize. When do you ever see successful people hanging around people who complain all the time? Why? These people criticize typically because of their own failures and insecurities. Remember that the enemy uses emotions that work together such as anger and fear. Not taking responsibility, ignoring your weaknesses, and projecting them onto other people through blame, jealousy, feeling superior, arrogance or anger. Negativity and anger are a good example of emotions that work together. These emotions can be helpful since they can make you make a stronger effort, especially when it comes to sports. Projecting your anger, such as blaming someone else, is not helpful.

One way to help control anger is through meditation, especially with some of the tapes available that can get you in a state you need to be in a short period of time that would typically take many hours to achieve. So when anger comes, meditation can help you recognize how you are feeling and be able to forgive yourself for feeling that way as well as understanding what is making you feel that way. Meditating will help you slow down to do this. Once this is understood, it will enable you to expand the built up energy into something that can help you such as working out and express it to someone who can help you and bring what you are feeling into perspective.

Remember that your mind is very open to new impressions when you wake up, so turning on negative news or reading negative news as soon as you awake is not a good idea. What does the media report on? That's right, negative news, and the more tragic the better. Instead, to put you in the right frame of mind, read an inspirational story, meditate, put on a show that makes you laugh. We are warned in the Bible about anger from Paul who wrote, "Do not grieve the Holy Spirit with whom you were sealed for the day of redemption.

Get rid of all bitterness, rage and anger, brawling and slander, along with every form of malice." I have to admit this is easier said than done.

I myself have this obsession with justice. I struggle many times throughout the day. Recently there was a car cutting everyone off in line. They got up to my car and the driver not only cut me off but one of the occupants threw a plastic soda bottle at my car. They then took off when the light just turned green, and I am grateful that this happened. They were young men about 20 with absolutely no muscle capacity to do a push up. Did I forget about it immediately – no way. I visualized how I might catch up to them and give them a beating, justifying in my mind that if I did so, they would learn a lesson and never do this to others again. Thank God I was not able to see them again. They could sue me and take everything I worked so hard for over the years, for someone who was not worth it. When you allow yourself to get deep into anger or rage the rational part of your mind gets cut off, and it goes to the part of the brain called the amygdala. The point in any situation is to be able to think of consequences or react rationally, but it is very difficult to do so when there is a chemical imbalance in your brain! The key is to be able to recognize how you are feeling and not let yourself get to the point where you are "cut off" from your ability to react rationally.

Sorry, I just got off track, please remember to be grateful for what you do have then go through a list of what you are grateful for. OK, to end this paragraph: a deep statement. Since we are all energy and all connected in some way, correct your behavior and influence your entire current circumstances.

FEAR. The worst thing a person could have in life when the end hits us all is regret. Knowing that you could have done something great in life but never took a chance. The emotion that prevents us from doing this is FEAR. This has to be number one when it comes to blocking almost everyone from success. What is fear? It is your thoughts about the future that create pain in your life. It is what you imagined and many times is not true. Overcoming your fear is a must if you want the prize. A great quote on fear is by Henry Louis Mencken who said, "The one permanent emotion of the inferior man is fear - fear of the unknown, the complex, the inexplicable. What he wants above everything else is safety."

We will get deeper into this subject, but the key is not to be afraid to make sudden or radical changes if an opportunity presents itself. It is important not to let fear override your faith. I am not saying making the decision based on your emotions, because you need to have careful consideration. If you doubt the wisdom of doing something, then be careful of taking radical change. It is said that when you are unsure of the vision of what you want, you need to spend a day or two in gratitude that you are actually getting it so that your mind is close to God so that when you make the decision, you will not doubt that it is the right thing.

Never rush, or enter into any venture if you have fear and doubt. We, as humans, want to conform to the norm, not to stand out too much. But you will never achieve anything great if you think "normally." The people who were doubted and ridiculed are the ones who created things that are great. Do I really need to give a list? Pause for a second and I am sure you can think of someone from the past who was told they were crazy, did not know what they are talking about, and maybe were even persecuted. This is why when you have that moment of clarity or an "ah-ha moment," the key is to act on it immediately, or it drifts of to a person willing to accept that gift. Sort of like the "memo" in *Jerry Maguire*. The attitude of gratitude so that you are close to your god, needs to be in place as other opportunities come in an increasing number.

I struggle with hurrying through things. When you find yourself hurrying, you need to step back, fix your thoughts on the outcome or things you want, and give thanks that you are getting it. The answer is Gratitude, which will strengthen your faith. Also, try to stay in the moment and not the future feeling guilty about past failures or regrets. An exercise that I like is to pick a time of day when you want to worry or fear something then move forward with your day. (Do not do this right before bed or early in the morning when you awake.)

Lastly, if you are not feeling motivated or positive, do not watch negative news or depressing movies. Tape things that make you laugh. Fear must be kept to a reasonable level because when you start to feel useless and unworthy then it can create permanent damage. When you have the negative feelings we are discussing, the key is to get rid of it just like you would with anything else in your life that causes you to be uncomfortable. This is going to sound confusing, but once again sometimes the emotion of fear or any other negative emotion is actually good to have and can push you to do things you do not want to do. But it is imperative for you to be able to use fear and negativity within reason and not let them create permanent damage. For example, when I was a mortgage broker, each month was wiped clear and I started all over again. Fear motivated me that I was able to do it last month but I was fearful that I might not be able to do it the next month. So, in fact, fear motivated me to push myself to come up with similar results.

The bottom line about fear is that it is a negative feeling that is the opposite of love. It is an energy that Evil thrives on. Evil does not thrive on love, forgiveness, and prayer. Lastly, please remember that neurons wire the brain through constant thoughts, so practice thoughts that are comforting. Just like when you are exercising or when you first learned to ski or ride a bike or if you bought a high performance sports car – you would not fill it with less than premium fuel. It is through repetition that things become second nature to us. The power to control thoughts is the most powerful thing an individual can do in life – period. This is written in the Bible when the apostle Paul wrote, "Whatever is true, whatever is noble, whatever is right, whatever is pure, whatever is lovely, whatever is admirable – if anything is excellent or praiseworthy – think about such things."

Meditation is the process of repeating a thought. This is why, as I stated earlier, it is an effective method of changing your life, like affirmations, the repetition is important. The problem today is that we have more choices than ever to get stimuli from many sources like the computer, TV, etc., and this has actually made us too weak or bored to focus our attention, especially on a constant thought.

Remember that fear will limit the range of action that you will take. Without fear you will live more fully and have more power and energy. Fear is used to control us today through the media and advertising of what could happen to you. Just go to the grocery store during a winter storm and you will find that person who buys five gallons of milk like they will be snowed in for weeks. We have this tendency to exaggerate the danger. As I write this, we are still not out of the recession with confidence. Yet compared to any time in our history, including the 1930s, we are safer and more secure than any moment in our history. Any race could really succeed in our nation, as evidenced with a black president, where less than 100 years ago, only the white males had that opportunity. Unlike today, females and those of any race have all of the same opportunities for success, too.

People, when they try to avoid fear, become paralyzed and do anything to avoid that fear, so they avoid the things that could advance their thinking. They think that by avoiding the task or risk it will bring comfort and keep the security they already have. I struggle with anxiety, but if we can overcome these fears we will have even more control of the things that we fear. Fear limits your actions, and takes away your power to shape events. Most people who seem to be "experts" have opinions on subjects with which they do not even have experience. Always be open minded and curious about things that are even contrary to what the "experts" say. This will lead to opportunity. God created us to be creative and independent individuals, and "experts" speaking conventional wisdom affect our subconscious by repeating things that may only seem to be true.

One of the fears that almost everyone must conquer is the fact that we are alone in this world. We have support, but the only person that has the power to change your circumstances is you. The key is to develop the attitude that you can manage any adverse condition or circumstance on your own. Please remember that fear is mostly based on past failure or experiences, and the vast majority of fear is predicated on things that never happen or are not real. The only way to overcome fear is action and future successes.

One last comment: we all gather together past memories, some that we do not want and store them in a warehouse inside our mind only to come out in times to limit our thinking or abilities. The key is to use this memory of stored negative images for our benefit. Sometimes these memories can be used to push us to greatness. How many times have you heard of stories of people who grow up with poor uneducated parents only for them to gain wealth, and become educated well-spoken adults. The pain or memory of being teased or ashamed could have pushed that individual to become the person they are today instead of being a victim and allowing their circumstances to give them excuses for living a life they do not want. The reason why we love designer materialistic items so much is because we believe that succeeding, have materialistic items, and wealth will make others love us, respect us, and have us feel a sense of pride. When pushing ourselves to succeed for these reasons we must be conscious of the potential pitfalls and not let ourselves be led astray.

It has never been easier for us to turn to drugs, either legal or illegal, to help us with our problems or feelings. There have never been more distractions to avoid our true feelings through recreational activities such as TV, computers, video games, etc. These are hard to resist, but once you entertain these distractions, it is very hard to leave because of the ease of avoiding reality. This is not the answer. In closing, the apostle John wrote, "There is no fear in love – perfect love casts out fear."

Do you ever talk to someone who is very needy? At times we want to say, "Do it yourself, why are you so pathetic and weak?" The ultimate goal is to gain that power of independence, and the only way to do this is through practice and effort. If we could only see the possibilities and the future, how this would erase our fears. People may curse the lack of resources that they have but do not see that this made them stronger or more creative. Things happen to us, and it is our minds that determine if they are bad or good. We all have a tendency to exaggerate minor setbacks as something larger than they really are. We all can look at past events to realize only later that it was not as bad as we thought it was. The key is to train your mind that this is just a challenge and actually an opportunity hidden. We all place limitations on what our minds can do. What you then think, then becomes your reality. There are many opportunities in life but you will hear sayings all the time that there are just a few opportunities that come our way in a lifetime where the opposite is true.

The key to controlling your fear is to reason and expect the fact that things happen for a reason and you must see the reason as a positive. If your wife has left you, perhaps that is the time to look at yourself to change so that you could mend the situation or you do not repeat the same mistakes. When you see a fearless person, people are naturally attracted to this feature. People will settle for things in life because they are afraid. Sometimes you do not see a person's aggression because it is passive. Usually these people will try to make it seem like they are the victim, when in reality they are the ones using techniques that are filled with hatred, such as using a child in a relationship or charging an unusual amount of money on a family credit card. Unfortunately, the only way these people respond is through power and for you to take bold steps that discourage this type of behavior. Once they see that things are not going their way they usually retreat. Also, when there are situations where you feel that injustice is happening to you, remain calm and patient and work behind the scenes. By making your case loudly so that you try to create public backing, you will find that you only make others mad as well. Another sign of fear is when a boss or spouse tries to control everything. It is a deep down sign of insecurity.

The past can drive your behavior, and it is based off of fear. It is your representation of past events, and forgetting the past and moving forward is one of the keys to success. The past continues to control most of our behavior. The fact is there is nothing you can do about your past. It is your belief in the future that is the most important thing. Also remember that it is not the event that causes stress but rather the emphasis we place on the situation we are in. The key here is no matter how bad the situation to think of something positive that will result from the situation. It is your thinking that stirs your emotions and what you focus on that matters. I will end this section as I have done others by stating control your thoughts and choose the life you want to live.

WORRY. Some people have asked me why I was able to be successful and in the past, I would use the word "worry." That by somehow worrying that I would not be able to somehow repeat my performance it would push me to try just as hard if not harder than what I did in the past. If I did not worry, I would lose my edge and become complacent and lazy. Did worry change things I could not change – so why waste the energy because it takes energy to worry? What worrying actually did was erode my confidence, took away my faith, and let go of the anxiety of trying to continue to repeat my success. By focusing my energy that I was going to "lose it all," if I did not stop it would have become a self-fulfilling prophecy. I have read in many books that if you concentrate on something long enough eventually it will happen to you. Since most of my thoughts were anxiety related, I made a conscious effort not to concentrate on something I do not want to attract.

CONTROL. We all have a tendency to try to control situations to our pleasing because of fear of change and chaos. We usually try to take aggressive actions to control the situation. By doing so when you try to force a response you tend to look defensive and weak. Typically, the harder we try to control the situation immediately we lose greater control in the long run. The key is to try to embrace these moments and look at them in a way that creates growth in character, and you can find a way to exploit the situation for a benefit. It is not what happens to us in life, it is how we react to things which counts.

One of the keys is to try to let go or not hold on to the bad emotion for a long time. Forgiving, or forgetting, is an emotion that everyone needs to master. They say not to sweat the small stuff and what that means is to live a balanced life. We cannot let ourselves get too excited or have extreme highs and also try to avoid extreme lows. When people see this they become attracted to you because you are that person they want in the foxhole during war, cool under pressure. You also need to avoid being the person whom everyone likes. What might seem as good behavior could be deep rooted fear of rejection.

There are, unfortunately, times where we need to be tough and fight for our rights or make difficult decisions. The fact is at times we must sometimes manipulate people and make ourselves look better than we sometimes are because, in the future, you will not have to act it out because you will actually become that person. The only control that you need to take over is your own behavior. This means taking responsibility, stop complaining, and stop blaming others for your failures. The most important controlled behavior you can try to master is to do things when you do not want to do them. Action is the key, even when you are unsure or do not feel like doing what must be done. Without action there is no chance for success. Never use failures as an excuse to stop trying. Sometimes we do not have control over our failures. We can only try to learn from them. Failures are only permanent when we stop trying. Faith is to keep trying when you have failed. Courage is to keep persisting when you or others have failed.

Part of my problem of control was that I would have to prove that I was right and that the other person was wrong. A lot of my problem with control deals with our own insecurity. You would think that successful people are secure, but the reason many have wealth and success is that they want approval from others, people to recognize their success and wealth and think they have control over situations they do not really have. Why do you think you see so many luxury cars on the highway? Just take away the emblems and switch it with another and many would abandon their cars for another.

Reflection is the key to all these emotions. Because without reflection we cannot change anything, especially things we do not want. That is why, for many, to truly change, something of a disaster or a devastating event needs to take place to say, "Wow! How did I let this happen, and I do not want this to happen again." Then, you search for ways to avoid this pain. The hope is that we find the answer in positive traits we wish to obtain. If not, we are prone to repeat our mistakes and do the same thing over and over again, which is, of course, the example of insanity. We need to consciously release our ailments, take responsibility, and give our negative personality traits to God. God gives us free will and will not magically do something for us that we choose not to have help with.

EXPECTATIONS. Unrealistic expectations. Another weakness of mine. We need to drop unrealistic expectations of our spouse, the government, employees, and friends and relatives. This is actually, as stated before, a national problem. Social Security has become a sense of entitlement. Humans are not God-like, meaning we easily make mistakes. So relying on someone else to fulfill our happiness or even to show that they appreciate us, in most cases, we will be let down. This was one of my biggest areas of mistakes. I relied on my wife for appreciation, and when she did not show it, it made me angry thinking she was selfish and spoiled. Instead, I needed to look at myself to provide my happiness. When it comes to being successful, people have an expectation or glorified thoughts of what a task, business, or job entails. They rarely see the sacrifice or the realization that most of the tasks to become successful are actually boring and repetitive. When you see the Olympic medalist having his name chanted, standing atop of the podium, we think how great it would feel. But rarely do we see the sweat and repetitive boredom that these individuals endured in order to get there.

If you are in sales, people might see the money or rewards but they do not see the number of rejections it took to get those results. If most people could see the sacrifice it takes, many would not attempt to try. You succeed when you can concentrate on the end results and have faith (one of the keys to overcoming your anxiety). Once the seed of success shows its head, then these boring tasks seem to become easier. You actually will then try harder at the tasks with a greater urgency. This is a skill that must be mastered. Avoiding being bored during routine tasks is actually a critically important skill that people often overlook. This was a particularly hard task for me to develop after graduating college when I had a lot of free time and when I was not wrestling. Just look to Thomas Edison or Walt Disney as examples of just two people who had countless experiments or bank visits to try to accomplish their goals.

All of us must master certain steps so that at the end it looks like we are gifted or that things come naturally to you. Our society of instant pleasure and wanting it now prevents us from achieving certain levels of success. Patience is a characteristic as well that we must possess. Patience to learn, to practice, to put up with failures, and to try again and put up with the drudge work and stop with the distractions. A lot of our expectations come from our ego which can never become controlled because, as human beings, we always want to grow and the ego will always want more.

Another deep thought is that when we have judgment against others it is a quality we see in ourselves. It is like the saying that you never noticed your car before until you wanted one or just purchased one. Many people put down behavior they are currently displaying because deep in their minds they have the same tendencies. The key is that when we notice ourselves feeling those behaviors that we dislike in others so much, we should then reflect on our own behavior. This could actually be a lesson or clue that you harbor to some degree the qualities in which you are judging people. If you do not acknowledge them you will always push them onto others and really never see your true self and improve so that those qualities will not surface especially in the worst of times.

The good news is that when we see someone whom we admire, those same qualities exist in us as well. It is the same way of being attractive in a quality another individual - that same quality exists in you. You can attribute this to movies. If a movie inspires you, then you possess that same quality. This is a very positive thing especially when you see this information in trying to succeed in your venue. The purpose of noticing qualities in others and ourselves is to be able to consciously change those patterns that we do not like. That is having control over our lives.

If you believe in a higher power, it is to feel secure that you are never punished but taught lessons to make us better people or prepared for our next success; the only person who does not wish you well is yourself. As stated repeatedly throughout this book, whatever we choose to think gives us the results we do or do not want. It is the way we think about things that makes a difference, the power, willingness, and strength to see how any circumstance can benefit us.

CONFLICT. Every conflict in our life has an opportunity, even when we do not see it in the beginning. There is typically a bigger purpose for this adversity or conflict. Many times during these tough times our true character is revealed.

They say that every marriage has some type of conflict and that it will never truly flourish or have a deep level of intimacy without it.

PRIDE. Another weakness. When I was arguing with my wife, my pride or want for respect would cause fights easily. It has to do with controlling another individual. I would be happy only when she agreed on my point of view, and when she would not, it caused me to attack her. It was truly exhausting. One of the traits that helped me was to try to put the other person's feelings above my own. The key is that when we fail to recognize our weaknesses, then we will never be able to get that breakthrough that we are seeking.

SACRIFICE. In order to get anything in life we have to be willing to give something up. Be it time, money, or materialistic wants. As time proceeds and success happens, we might think that our sacrifice would have paid off so that we would not want more. But one of the biggest roadblocks to success is the I WANT IT NOW MENTALITY. We talked about the right mentality, but having the right mindset is not the whole picture, action is necessary too. The only time when true change is implemented is when there is pain. Comfort is the fall of people who have potential. Many people will quit when they see that their comfort is disappearing. The few do whatever it takes to experience abundance. I guess it is the same in sports. You hear stories of gymnasts who are at the gym at 5:00 a.m. while most of us at that age where sleeping. A story that I remember reading about was that Caesar, in trying to conquer Britain, when he landed, burned the ships and said, "Now it is win or perish."

CALMNESS. I still have not yet achieved this in my own personal life, but it is what all of us are trying to achieve. It is sometimes referred to as serenity. It is also referred to as the journey of a long and patient effort to self-control. It is at this moment when you can look at life and situations and see how you react to things and the cause and effect of your behavior. It is here where we tend less to worry or fear things but to be more poised, calm, and serene in times of struggle and conflict. Being calm can lead to more success because people prefer to deal with an individual who has an even calmer demeanor. It is a sign of self-control. This does not mean weakness, it means being strong but calm. Leadership during major stress such as on the battlefield in war is a perfect example of this character trait. The person is loved, respected, and revered. I am a person who has soured my life, and there are many people in my exact position, because of an explosive temper. It can destroy character and sometimes ruin all that they have worked for. It all comes back to self-control.

Self-control is real strength and calmness is power. Control your thoughts and you will master your destiny. Emergencies will happen and you will take care of them when they do appear. Sometimes when planning for your emergencies, it affects your actions today. So, just be concerned with doing today's work the best you can. Too many people concern themselves with huge obstacles that never come. I am not saying ignore them. When you see them coming make plans to avoid them. The key to calmness in any business venture from a mental standpoint are the following rules:

Never speak about yourself or your affairs in a discouraging way. Small people talk about others while big people think about ideas. The middle class talk about toys they can obtain.

Never speak in a way that admits a possibility of failure. Never speak of times that are hard, including recessions, or business conditions being unsure or doubtful. (When other people are going through a tough time, you will find great opportunities.) I must also add complaining. I REALLY struggle with this. My mother was a positive person but had a habit of complaining. I have to continuously remind myself that the more you complain about something the more likely it will show up in your life. Many people who are more successful than me are not complainers and do not whine about things.

Think of complaining as cursing yourself or putting a spell on yourself because you actually are doing this. One good thing in analyzing myself is that I might offset the complaining because I am very grateful for everything in my life and this is one of the great keys for getting what you want.

Always think about advancement in the future. The middle class is easily impressed with fortune and fame, just look at the magazine sales that show pictures of stars and what they are doing. Continue to act in a certain way and when things turn out to be a failure know that these failures were merely stepping-stones to better things.

Gratitude unifies God with the mind of men. Form a clear picture of the things you wish to have and be thankful like you've already received this gift. Frequently think of this picture, have the faith and gratitude of receiving this gift. Do all that you can do daily to achieve your goal, and through your thoughts and faith, you will attract the people and things to assist you.

Lastly, do not complicate things. A great example of this is when it comes to losing weight. There are great helpful facts that could speed the process tremendously when it comes to dieting and exercise that cannot be denied. But you do not need to know everything - the key is to take action. I will tell you in one short sentence how to lose weight. Are you ready? Here it is: Eat less and move more. I am not saying not to get facts. It is extremely important especially when opening up a business, but too many people become paralyzed by the facts and never take any action. They know too much but do too little. Here is another secret to having a comfortable retirement. Are you ready? Here it is: spend less than what you make.

Calmness is contagious. If people are in a panic, everyone gravitates to the individual who is calm. Repeating your problems or worries is contagious and makes everyone nervous. A belief in a higher calling is very powerful because you have a sense of being helped and that you are not alone. I have a problem controlling my anger, and they say that 'people who get angry easily are poor emotionally." I have been that way for years.

CHANGE. It is continuous and it shows your personality when change reveals itself. Pay attention the next time when change rears its ugly head and try to evaluate your behavior. I myself had a tendency to get frustrated, angry, and would complain. Looking back, at times I believe it revealed my worry, lack of faith, and deep rooted anger. Change happens and we get worried. For many of us change creates more effort; it is something we worry about, and we are not sure if we can handle the change. We can go back to FEAR – what I talked about earlier. We question our strength, so instead of accepting it, we waste a lot of energy trying to fight it, so the change becomes harder. The key here is to have faith that the change is for our benefit. This might be the most important thing I can tell you throughout this whole book. The only way to be truly secure is to TAKE risk. It will get you out of the 9-5 rat race that you will be in for the rest of your life. I had a tendency to jump into things, but I have learned to educate myself before making the decision and you must always look at the true worst case scenario and be willing to accept the consequences.

The biggest problem of many in the middle class is that they might take a chance, and if they fail, they never try again. I've always believed that we should read at least two autobiographies a year of successful people and one common thing you will notice is that they have failed many times. So the middle class will play the game of life not to win but just trying not to lose, and the fear of change and loss is the motivating factor. There is no way to succeed unless you are able to control these two emotions. It is true that wisdom comes with age, and from my talks with many clients at the end of their lives, there is the regret of not spending more time with the family and not taking more risk to go after their dreams. Also, the bad times were not as bad as they seemed at the time. With no risk there is no opportunity to have a true sense of security to have the freedom we all desire and which made America great.

LOVE. This is really the underlying feeling that all of us seek. Why become that great athlete, make a certain amount of money or own that car? If you break it down, it all comes down to the desire to be loved. Social connections are the most important thing in peoples' lives. That is why isolation for prisoners is one of the worst punishments you could give an inmate.

We need to respect people and realize that people are doing the best they can. I had the tendency in the past to be too hard on my employees and tell them what they were doing wrong instead of complimenting them on what they were doing right. There is wisdom in making people feel important and praising them.

Part Two: Money

Boy, when it comes to money, almost all of us are associated with greed. In the movie *Wall Street*, Gordon Gecko said, "Greed is good." Yet, greed is responsible for the bubble not only in the stock market but in the housing bubble that just burst as well. But the fact is that without it, in our civilized society, you cannot survive. If somebody tells you that money is not important, I can tell you that you are speaking to a broke person. In reality, money is everything in this world. Money can help people if you want to give it. Money determines the home you live in, the school your kids could attend, the vacations you have, where you eat, shop, and, more importantly, how you can spend your time - especially if you do not have to work in the 9-5 rat race.

While I would also consider myself a pretty good father, a decent husband, pretty good athlete in my day... make no mistake about it, all of those things matter. Nevertheless, money is and will always be a very important aspect of anyone's life, regardless of their attributes and achievements. Once you are able to get financial concerns out of your list of worries, so that it is really not an issue in your life anymore, then you have the ability to concentrate your efforts and attention on other IMPORTANT things.

Certainly it's true that money is not going to bring you happiness. A better marriage might make you a better person, that is true, but these types of people are rich and poor alike. Being happy is a choice, a state of mind, but if you have to choose being rich and happy, or happy and poor, which one would you choose?

The way that you spend your money really tells a lot about your character. You can be rich but do not pay your bills or you spend your money continuously on unnecessary or outrageous things such as having a bath in Perrier water, which is no better than most tap water. What money will do is make people take notice of you, and if you act inappropriately, it compounds a situation.

Think about being rich in your town and well known but you never tip your waiter. If they know you have money, it makes matters ten times worse. Money attracts attention, and it can also make you irresponsible. Think about Michael Jackson. His money essentially killed him because some people, when attracted to money, will do anything an individual wants even though it might not be in their best interest. Money will give you peace of mind, more freedom, and perhaps more time. And if you're a jerk, it will make you seem even more jerky, believe it or not.

Also, money does not care how educated you are. In fact, 85 percent of self-made millionaires do not have a college degree. Be careful not to think that what you do for a living always determines how much money you have at the end. To some degree, this is true, but I believe anyone can be wealthy with discipline and time. Let me give you an example. I grew up lower middle class. My father has a sixth grade education and was so poor that he did not even have shoes. He slept with his brothers and sisters in one room with one bed and there were seven of them. My mother graduated from high school and her parents rented their whole life. One of the things that I wanted to do in life was to go to college. I thought that by going to college I would make more money, so I did. Then I went into the military because I thought it would make me more valuable to an employer, and it would also help pay for my Master's degree. And by getting my Master's degree I could ultimately make more money...

Well, while I was working at a bank, my job used to be cutting the checks to all the wealthy people. We were forbidden to ask personal questions on how they accumulated their wealth. We all have this prejudice. Whenever I saw a doctor or lawyer coming in, I would assume they have the wealth because of their degrees and what they do. But when I saw the normal small business owner, the construction worker, or dry cleaner, the tellers and I would sometimes even make up stories. "I heard his father was rich, and he got an inheritance," or "I heard he won a lawsuit." It was not until Bill walked into the bank when my assumptions changed to some degree. I was about to close the bank and go to Happy Hour. As I was about to lock the door, Bill knocked on it while I was literally turning the key, so I thought, "Son of a gun, I have to let him in."

Now Bill was a mechanic and owned his own little gas station, but I believe he missed his calling in life because he was one funny individual. And I believe he really tried hard to be funny that day because he mostly sensed that I did not want to be there. I felt very comfortable around him, and I was *about to graduate from grad school soon, so if the manager of the bank fired me I really did not care. Therefore, I decided to ask him, point blank, how he created his wealth of $1.6 million at the age of 58. I asked him how he had so much money and whether he got an inheritance or won a lawsuit or something. He stated to me that his older brother, 10 years older, said to save 10% of what he made and he had been doing so since the age of 18 when he started working for the individual who eventually sold him his shop. He said it happened to be about $800,000 about five years ago, and it happened to double in value in the last five years which enabled him to retire.*

I could not comprehend that someone who never made more than $60K a year could accumulate this amount in savings, plus have a free and clear four bedroom home! So the last few weeks of that job, I started to ask other people and, indeed some had an inheritance or won a lawsuit, but the majority of them were just great disciplined savers.

Did I listen to their pearls of wisdom? No, when I graduated and finally got a job, I bought a flat screen TV and a new utility vehicle that I could barely afford the payments on, which became old and did not look as good as it did when I drove it off the lot. I made the usual mistakes. But after that, I became a good, disciplined saver and sought wealth through mentors and became self-employed. Some folks think that people who have money have earned it dishonestly, and yes, there are people who have earned their wealth this way but it is not the majority. Just like Bill the mechanic, you can carve out an honest living and still become a millionaire by responsible saving.

God wants you to have wealth. Any god in almost any religion wants the best for His people. Do you really think that God wants you to be poor? A great way of living is that every time you feel you are worrying then practice letting go of the need to control the outcome. Also, if you have a certain passion for things, those desires could be a gift that God wants for you. God created the "stuff" that you desire…God created beauty, so thank God for creating such beauty. But if purchasing the item creates debt that you cannot afford to carry and causes you to worry more and not to be as generous because of it, then it was not a good purchase.

Do you notice how God seems distant when we have negative feelings like sadness, worry, or anger? This is why controlling your thoughts is so important, so that when God gives you an opportunity you can actually receive the gift. Not controlling your thoughts makes your reactions automatic and you continue to have the same results. The way we live is a reflection of what we are thinking. Your mind cannot be in two places at the same time, so think great thoughts and pay attention to what you are thinking. Either the thought is leading you towards God and greatness, or it is not.

Also, it is not what you earn that matters the most, it is what you keep. Finding ways to save money or spend your money more wisely is just as important as working hard to make more money. If you think about it, it is really the same thing. Both lead to keeping more money in your pocket.

Who is better off? Someone who makes a thousand dollars and spends $500 on a widget he will not use, or a person who makes $700 but only spends $200 on the widget? Learning to save and act thoughtful with your money will allow you to have less stress and live life more purposefully to get what you really want out of life.

Ways you can save money or be wiser with your money? Here are some things you can do.

- When you need a rental car, do not rent one at the airport (which can be more expensive), take a cab, or rent one at a nearby rental location. When you rent a car do not be afraid to ask for freebees like a GPS system. Sometimes they will throw it in for free. Make sure you ask for specials they are having. Also by belonging to an organization like AARP can save you money when renting a car.

- Do not buy a new car. Buy a one or two-year old car with low mileage. Go online and look up the value of the car on cars.com or Kelly Blue Book. Also, get your loan from your bank or credit union unless you qualify for the dealership's special promotions such as 0% financing. Do not trade in your car to the dealer, sell it yourself. A lot of time you think they are giving you a better deal, but all they are typically doing is taking a discount on the car they are selling you. Remember, they have to make a profit off that car, so you would be better off selling it yourself. The days of haggling are over because now you can find people to haggle for you. Where? Online like companies like the American Automobile Association's car buying service. Just let them know what car you want and they do the rest. And when you do buy, you can check your car on Autocheck, which can email you a report on the vehicle just by giving them the VIN number located on your vehicle. I have bought a few vehicles in the past from rental companies that turned out to be a great buy. Companies like Avis, Budget, Dollar, and Enterprise advertise online.

- Keep track of your spending. Do it just for a month. By keeping track of your spending, you will see what you are spending your money on and how you are able to save.

- If you want a better rate on your savings account at the banks, do not go to your local or national banks in town. Go to banks online like ING that offer much better rates and sometimes even better services, many times because their costs are lower because they do not have to maintain a building and additional costs associated with it.

- Credit cards. PLEASE shop around. Go online to sites like lowcards.com to compare interest rates. Also, call your existing credit card company and tell them you want a better rate and let them know of the companies you are comparing them with. If they do not lower it, close your account and leave. (Make sure you speak with a supervisor).

- If you are self-employed or if your company has a Health Savings Account (HSA), take advantage of it. You fund the account with pre-tax dollars and if used for health purposes, it is tax free. You also can carry over your benefits and dollars from year to year.

- Fitness gyms. How gyms really make their money is having you as a member for years. They usually have first time membership fees. If a rival gym is having a special you could show it to the gym you are thinking of joining and ask them to match the offer. You will be surprised that many times they will take your discounted offer in a heartbeat.

- When buying real estate, if possible always put down 20%. Why? PMI Insurance. Try to put down 20% and if you are not able to, then when your house is 78% Loan to Value (LTV) - as long as you made your payments on time - make sure they remove the insurance. Which means if you only put down 10% on a $100,000 mortgage your house is 90% LTV. Over time you pay down your mortgage and your house usually appreciates.

- Never take an extended warranty. Enough said.

- If you have a gift card use it right away because it does not mean that the company has to accept it if they go bankrupt.

- Check your credit report for free. The credit reporting agencies are required to give you one free credit report a year. Equifax, Experian, and Trans Union. Go online at annualcreditreport.com or mail your request to Annual Credit report Request Service at P.O. Box 105281,

Atlanta, GA 30348; Toll Free Number 877-322-8228. Why do this? Because of errors. I have found four errors the last five years on my credit report. One of the agencies might not have the error which is why you check all three. If you find the error, then use the correction forms that they provide on their websites. To help with your credit, try to keep balances low. Not maxing out any one card. Also, believe it or not, do not close out all cards. Especially ones that you have paid on a timely basis. Try to put at least a small charge on each card and then pay it off every year so that the credit card companies will not cancel the card for you. Do this only as a way to keep your score high. The other things, unless it is an error, you cannot control, such as past payment history, amounts that you owe, and the length of your credit history.

- I threatened to leave my cable company for satellite and they reduced my rate. If they had not, then I would have switched. Always speak to a supervisor if possible.

- Ask existing telephone companies for a better deal - especially unlimited calling for no more than about $20. Look at alternative long distance carriers you've never heard of before, such as Pioneer and Unitel. If you make your calls over the Internet, use services like Vonage or the cheapest I can find is Skype.

- Book your airline seats for your family one at a time. Always use the Internet for the best deals instead of calling. Also look for companies like Hotwire and Orbitz if you are having a hard time finding cheap tickets.

- When you book a hotel room, make it a habit a few weeks to call the hotel a few days before you are about to arrive to see if there are any specials or if you can get a better price.

- Use Internet sites for all your travel booking needs. Some companies with local agencies in town have a higher overhead. One company that I use is Friendly Planet which is very cost efficient. On a trip to India for myself and my wife, it saved me about $8,000 in comparison to a local travel agent.

- Get your credit in order. Cut down on consumer debt and pay them on time or better yet early. Pay off auto loans early. Avoid using more than 50% of your credit line.

- Let's get real for a second – I bet when I say most of the following ideas to you, your response will be along the lines of that it's impossible to do. Bullcrap – if you were forced to take away some of these luxuries to move you closer to your goal, isn't it worth it? Here are some desperate measures, but by doing so, they will put you in the fast zone for saving money to help you get where you want to be. You will survive...

- Buy a cheaper car. The only thing that will hurt you is your own ego. I would rather make $200 car payments than $600. >Give up your high speed Internet connection. If you do not use it for your livelihood, then all you need is a little more patience.

- Give up your home phone and use just your cell. Also look at your plan and see if you can save money on it.

- Get rid of your extra premium channels like HBO or Starz. You are going to be too busy anyway during these times creating wealth.

- Look at the insurance you are paying. Combine your home and car insurance together. Raise your deductibles.

- Stop eating out! Enough said. And when you do shop, the store's no-name toilet paper will do the same job as the brand name version. Also, always shop with a budget and list because you really do not need those Fritos, even if your taste buds crave them and your stomach rumbles at the sight of them!

- Get all the stuff in your house that you do not really need and have a yard sale. Sell to consignment shops. Post your stuff on bulletin boards. I like this activity a lot because if you want to take control of your life, you need to clean out the clutter. It is amazing how good you feel about yourself when you really clean out your house, your car, fix things that needed to be fixed, get that haircut, clean those clothes, etc. When you get these things out of your way, it makes you feel like you are then ready to take on bigger challenges without getting caught up on the small stuff. This should really be one of the first steps for people who want to seize control over their lives.

- Carry cash. This exercise helped my wife. It seemed like when I gave her that credit card, it wasn't like real money. But when I gave her that lump sum in cash instead of credit, it made her think twice when she was about to buy something and actually made the money last longer.

- OK, this is not about saving money, but make your kids earn the money before you just give it to them. They will come to respect money a lot more and it will help them become better consumers. It will show them responsibility and actually shows love because you are teaching them about money. Especially if you take part of it and invest it for them and show them why you are doing so – Bill would be proud. Then let them track it and educate them. Lessons learned will be repeated.

The fact is that many of us try to use money to impress others. We yearn for respect and want to impress others. We need to be content. The problem is that when we buy these items we feel excited at first but then that excitement goes away and we feel guilt. The key is to have guilt-free enjoyment. We are shallow in our beliefs, and it really has to do with insecurity and wanting to belong. It is like high school all over again, wanting to belong to a group that is respected. Patience is really the key here. I believe moving into a new home when you have debt to take care of is a bad idea, because with that new home the probability of paying off that debt diminishes dramatically. Most of all, it will not change unless it is a deep hurt that moves us to change. The key is to get mad, really angry, and so fed up that it stirs you to change for the better. The first step of anyone getting their act together is to add up all their assets and then add up everything you owe, then you have a real idea of where you're at.

You need to know where your starting point is. If you skip this step, then throw away the book right now. This information will really give your life direction. Then the next step is to develop goals to get you there.

- If you have no goals, you will not know what direction to go. It is like driving without any place in mind. Just randomly cruising, and you'll get lost. Find out what you really want in life and write it down. It does not matter if it seems impossible –that's all in your mind and can be overcome, as explained in the Mentality section.

- Then start a budget. Yes, a budget. It does not make a difference how much you make. How is it possible that Mike Tyson who would make over $40 million for one fight went bankrupt? Or a hairdresser I know who never made over $30,000 a year, yet can retire with two million dollars? I will again reference the most popular book in the world that states, "which of you intending to build a tower does not sit down and count the cost if you have enough to finish it?"

Developing a budget is telling your money what direction you want it to go. While it might sometimes feel like money is in control of your destiny, you are truly its master and it needs to be told what to do. One of the keys to getting rich and ahead in life, as I stated earlier, is to carry cash and pay with cash only. This will make you think twice before spending. I have tried this and it really works! Cash also helps you get bargains and discounts from store owners. Trust me, the next time you go into a store and tell them you can charge this or pay cash, but with cash you want a discount; you will be surprised by what the store will do for you so they can save on the credit card transaction fees.

Always have an emergency fund so when unexpected things come your way, and they always do, you will be prepared to stick to your goals. That is what an emergency fund is all about - the ability to keep moving towards where you want to be without getting off track. Just remember to always replenish the emergency fund when you have the ability to do so. Three months of monthly bills saved with two working spouses, six months with only one source of income from one individual. There is always a way out. Debt management companies like CCs are not the answer; it is just like declaring Chapter 13 bankruptcy. This is about changing your habits instead of doing the same things that got you into this situation to begin with. A 'BK' will stay with you forever.

The key to making it out of the hole and staying out of debt forever is firstly making a list of your debts, tackling each one, one at time, and paying the minimum amount on the rest. This will give you the sense of accomplishment as you see your debt disappearing. Continue to do this and it will be like a big snowball gathering momentum every time you pay something off because it frees up more money and larger dollar amounts to pay the next bill off and so on and so on.

Debt, I believe, except for a home that you can easily afford, is not a good thing. So, that's why you want to stay within the lines of your budget and diminish your debt, to make you as rich as possible as quickly as you can. How does this tie into being wealthy? Think about it for a moment. You cancel all your debt – what's left to pay? Just the things you cannot avoid that are recurring, such as your electric and food bills. You then have all this free cash to invest in a business, real estate or investments. Then the money starts working for you to create more money, which allows you to invest in more investments.

Time Management

If we really take a look at our time, we will see that we all have a little extra time to create wealth. There are so many statistics on how much time people spend in front of a TV, sleeping, on the Internet, etc. If we can just spend some of that time on things that will move us closer to our goals instead of away from them, many more people would succeed such as taking a class, or reading something that can help create wealth. The fact is success does take hard work and how you spend your time either brings you closer or further away from your goals. There are so many success stories of people who emigrated from foreign countries, worked several jobs and are millionaires today.

Becoming wealthy is a choice, and I am assuming by reading this book, it is a choice that you want available to you. Some people do not care to be rich because of prior, deep rooted, subconscious beliefs so they do not care to be wealthy. By the way, these people blame circumstances from their spouses, backgrounds, skin color, education, religion, you name it. It is easier to blame others than to blame themselves. But it is mostly because there are no written goals, integrity issues, lack of responsibility, perhaps low self-esteem or discipline. My wife is a great person, one of the kindest people you will ever meet, and when I first met her every time I saw her she looked like a millionaire but did not have two pennies to rub together. Her priorities were not where they should have been. She could find money to buy name-brand clothes, but could not find money to save for her child's college before I met her.

Thus, the first key to having wealth is to: 1. Find out what you owe and write it down. 2. Develop a plan that is written down, so you can follow it.

Where do you get a plan? Some points will be simple like cutting unnecessary expenses; other points will be added to the list by educating yourself with books like this and by emulating other people who have created wealth.

Let's talk about cutting expenses, like eliminating credit cards. Trust me, if you really had to, you could survive. Going to a credit counselor is the same as going bankrupt. Instead, save the expense and call the credit card companies yourself and tell them about your situation. Ask to set up a reduced rate, lower the amount due. You will be surprised how quickly they will do it, because if you go bankrupt, they get nothing. So, you actually have more options than you might think. Once you start the program, live by it.

Where to Find Money!

Yes, I said 'find' money. There are places that will help you to start a business, or even help you during tough times and it does not cost you anything. It is true, and too many people do not take advantage of these simple tips. Guess what, I am going to give them to you, and I promise there has to be one idea that you can use here to find money you never thought you had or get it for free. Here is my list of money-finding tips:

1. Too many of us have savings bonds. It is what people bought for us when we were children to help later on in life. The problem is that many of us forgot about these bonds, or our parents forgot about them. There are billions of dollars in cash that is unclaimed. Billions! So take five minutes of your time get online at www.savingsbonds.com and check the individual section and put in your social security number. If you find some, all you have to do is download the forms you need and send them in. (By the way – check your parents' account; I found $800 for my dad and $1,500 for my mother.)

2. Bank Accounts – same thing. It is amazing but again it is worth five minutes of your time. Go to www.unclaimed.com/lost_account.htm

3. Call the FDIC at 1-877-275-3342 to find out if you or your parents have any CD's that were never claimed. You will be amazed at the number of people that do not have any details of where their assets are.

4. Many times people are owed money from the government and are not even aware that a refund is due to them. Why not check by calling 800-829-1954. Especially if you or someone moved. The IRS will not forward to the new address.

5. Make sure your CPA is aware of all these. Otherwise, he is just a tax preparation machine. There is a Child Tax Credit if your children are under the age of 17, a nice $1,000 per child; a first time home buyer credit up to $8,000; and an education tax credit up to $1,800 per student. If you are thinking about solar energy for your house, you can get a credit up to 30% of the cost. If you want to be educated about tax credits or to receive assistance preparing your tax returns, you could get some help from an organization called "Ladder Up" which will help you prepare your taxes or actually prepare your taxes for you.

I can go into some details about these credits and tell you income restrictions, but you first need to see if you are eligible for these programs. If so, take advantage of them because they can save you thousands of dollars. For most, all it will take is to write down and make sure your CPA is applying these credits. If you cannot afford a CPA, then Google the organization Ladder Up for help.

6. Being self-employed means owning real estate, a side business, or inventing a product. You can earn $600 if you hired a veteran, another tax credit. If I had a magic wand, I would have everyone be self-employed to a degree.

7. As we get older, one thing that it seems most of us need, or get advised to take, is prescription drugs. This for many can be very expensive. What most people do not do though is take advantage of some of these great organizations such the Partnership for Prescription Assistance (www.pparx.rg) or freementalhealth.com. You may call them at 888-477-2669. There are many others. Three organizations that I am aware of besides the above are: www.needymeds.org, www.familywise.com and www.healthwellfoundation. States even offer discounted drug programs. Also, believe it or not, you can actually reduce your cost by just asking. I remember I had no insurance one time because I was between jobs, and by actually talking to the doctor, I set up a repayment plan with him for a cost lower than what the actual fee was. A stupid mistake when I was young was that I should have taken advantage of COBRA that lets you use your old policy from your ex-employer for a certain period of time. But the point is you actually have some bargaining power here. The health care system in America is not as bad as the news organizations and politicians claim. Again, go to that great invention called the Internet and look up these organizations. There is financial aid for many diseases, from heart disease to cancer, as well as vision care. www.findahealthcarecenter.hrsa.gov will help in that search.

8. Grants. There is a grant for almost everything. But the majority of us do not take advantage of any grants. I know I did not until I picked up a book and educated myself. Boy, really think about this one. The good old politicians love to hide things in these bills that have nothing to do with the actual bill. It is sort of like me saying to you, "OK, Jim, I will vote for your bill to fix up the roads, but I need a grant to help

out my pig farmers in Iowa." That's politics. The problem is that most people are clueless regarding what is available to them except a few that the politicians publicized. By the way, do grants need to be paid back? No! Ok, I will list a few to look into, if relevant to you: first time home buyers, phone services, child services, clothing services, working moms, volunteers, home improvements, mentoring, farmers, etc. It does NOT make a difference what field you are in, or what business you want to start up, search for a grant that can help. Try www.fdcenter.org or www.govbenefits.gov (This has a quick search button that will narrow down your search) or www.grants.gov, For non-profits, go to www.guidestar.com.

Run your life and career like a well-oiled machine - Keys to efficiency:

1. To get the ball rolling, everyone should straighten out their homes, cars, and work space. Throw away everything that you do not really need, fix things that are broken, and dust and clean. This will help give you a sense of control and order to your life, and will allow you to have some early success with getting your life together. It will reduce your stress, and allow you to concentrate on things that bring you closer to your goals, instead of having a cluttered life (and a cluttered mind).

2. As I've previously covered at length, write down your goals. This is a MUST DO exercise: Simply write down a goal in these areas of what you really would like to achieve in each one of these areas: Spiritual goal, Health goal, spousal goal, family goal, adventure goal, educational goal, career goal, financial goal and travel goal. Learn to identify what is really the most important thing. Then just concentrate on the things that are the most valuable and the better you will become while taking less time to accomplish them and the more polished you will become. The real key to this point is to stop doing the things that are of low value. If it takes you one hour to get a client who makes you $4,000 and one hour to do the paperwork, then delegate the paperwork to someone at $15 an hour so you can spend that hour with another $4,000 prospect. Most people are too blind to see this point and think they are saving money by doing so, when in reality it is costing them money. If you were to look at an individual's day, most of the time is wasted on activities that do not bring much value. The key to remember is "what is the most valuable use of my time at this

point?" then do it. It feels uncomfortable, especially if it is a difficult task, but people need to push themselves through it because it feels much better than avoiding it. Do the critical things first.

3. Do not overlook an individual directly if they cannot benefit you directly. It is important to know if they can introduce you to people who you need to speak with. Work with people or hire people who are the opposite of you or have abilities and skills that you do not possess. Too many people lack the decisiveness to make a decision. Stick with your decisions.

4. Always have a list. There is just too much to remember in a day without writing it down and checking it off. It keeps you on track, it helps you to remember, and it just feels good to check things off creating a sense of accomplishment. Planning activities the night before should not be overlooked. Remember it programs your subconscious mind and gets it ready for the day ahead of you.

5. If running your own business, do not have everyone doing the same task. Assign the responsibility to one person then cross train someone else in case that person is no longer available to do the task.

6. For organizing your home and office space so that it is a safe haven making you more productive, there is the garbage can. That's right; get rid of old clothes, paperwork, etc.

7. Keep a pen and paper next to your bed. Typically when you are relaxed, ideas come to mind that can change your life. That is why I believe that meditation is important as stated earlier.

8. Listen to books in the car when you drive to work. Keeps your mind active and stimulated.

9. This is the strongest trait that I have: I have a huge sense of urgency. To a fault. So many people I know have no sense of urgency, so things never get completed or they do, but by the time they complete their task, I have done three times what they have accomplished. Thus I become more successful. Action is the most important trait that separates the successful person from the unsuccessful person. It ties into self-discipline, to do the things that you really do not want or feel like you want to do.

10. Admire and look up to people who are wealthy and successful because what you admire or respect you are most likely to gravitate towards. They became successful for a reason.

11. Know your net worth. Add all your bills and debts and subtract them from your assets to determine your net worth.

12. Exercise. It is a stress reliever, creates extra energy, makes you look better, and you will be happier.

13. Pay other people to do things around the house or at work so it could free up your time. You have to look at your time as being valuable. I can do the paperwork for investments myself, but it might take me two hours. If I pay someone $20 an hour that would cost me $40 or I can sell a few investments, make some calls, meet with a client and make thousands.

14. Avoid procrastination! Take action and force yourself to get started. Most people want things but never take action. When you procrastinate, it might feel good for the short term but in the end, it leads do discouragement.

15. Use visualization. It is the key to keeping you excited and focused. It is one of the keys for attracting things, including wealth and success. Visualize to music specifically for meditation use.

16. I believe this statement is huge. DO THE THING YOU FEAR THE MOST FIRST. Your day will be more fulfilled and this will give you energy to do the other things that need to be done. When you do the thing that you fear the most first, it relieves anxiety, and it inspires you. So target things you really do not want to do such as make that tough phone call, approach that person you don't want to deal with, and watch your confidence, energy, and stress relief soar. Typically, the thing we fear the most is one of the most important things that needs our attention. Do not delegate this task since that is the easy way out. Take personal responsibility.

17. Read about others. No fiction books, but rather autobiographies on people who have struggled and overcome odds to succeed in their endeavors.

18. To some degree, what I know is that if you are able to sell, you will never go hungry. Communication is very important in not only our profession but in our personal life. This is an area where I am both very good at and bad at simultaneously. I mean that in my personal life, or when dealing with conflict, my communication skills can be lacking at times. There are many books on this subject, but what I can tell you is that this is what I believe has helped me. In times when I am frustrated, I use nonverbal cues that are not advisable and can be learned as a lesson for you of what not to do. They are rolling your eyes, fidgeting, shaking your head, or showing signs of wanting to say something. There are also verbal mistakes of using sarcasm saying such things as "give me a break" or using "you always" or "never," like I say to my wife. Also, interrupting or not addressing the issue at hand and instead distracting the person by changing the subject are hindrances to the communication that is taking place. Instead, if you can remember to remain calm and not to use verbal cues and nonverbal cues and instead just try the following, you will be much more effective in what you are trying to get across:

   A. Always make sure, especially if it is important in business and your personal life, to find out what time is convenient for the person to talk and also how long it will take.

   B. When they are talking to you, make sure that you are not using verbal or nonverbal cues and to show that you are listening and validate what they are saying by repeating important points of what they are telling you.

   C. You also always want to know what people think about a subject before approaching them. If I have a client who for some unknown reason does not like variable annuities, I do not mention this to them at the time. It is only when you strengthen a relationship with an individual through time that can you then go back and have them be willing to listen. If you do not know what they are feeling about a certain matter, ask them.

   D. I always repeat myself to them about what they are telling me, I also repeat the solution to what they have been telling me is their concern or what they desire.

E. Try to tell a story of what you are trying to express and be sure to use emotions when possible.

F. If I am in a hurry with someone who might be a prospect for one of my businesses or investment ideas and I do not have enough time or the atmosphere is not conducive to conduct business, then I try to create a sense of curiosity without giving them the solution. This way, they will at least listen to your idea. For example, after listening, you say, "What if I could show you something that will help you with this ____ or help solve this ____ or help you with _____, would you be interested?" Then set a time when you could talk about it or show them the solution. This is not a book on communication, but these are just some tips that if you included everything I have been saying from A-F your chances of exceeding with others is greatly enhanced.

STATISTICS

Let's start off with some facts.

1. There are over four million households that have a million dollar net worth.

2. ????

INVESTING

Before we discuss investing, we have to understand why money is so important. First, it helps create a lifestyle that is desirable and fulfilling. Second, it provides financial independence. Lastly, it can provide good for the community and be used to benefit others including your children and loved ones.

Let's face the facts, like reading or writing, learning about investing is something that requires education. There is a great quote by Benjamin Franklin that states, "If you think education is expensive, try ignorance." By the way, please learn from people who are successful. I do not care if they are educators, advisors, truck drivers, pizza shop owners, sanitation owners. etc. I blew off an individual who was a high school drop out and stated he owned a sanitation company only to find out he was worth millions and earned more than a 100 trucks throughout the area I lived.

One basic concept to remember, which is very simple, is buying a depreciable asset is spending but buying appreciable assets is investing. I would surely bet that 70% of what we purchase we do not need and are assets that depreciate. Do not get me wrong, the purpose is not to save every penny which is not the key to living a balanced life. Another basic principle is that you must avoid the addiction of having/spending more than you can afford. You need to have the mentality of using money to attract more, then the material rewards will eventually be inevitable.

We have heard this a thousand times, but it is still the truth. You need to save 10% of what you make. It is the only way to create passive income through investments later when you retire. I have seen people who make over $500,000 a year and people who make $50,000 a year who spend exactly what they make. It does not make a difference what you make; it's what you keep that counts. Many professionals including doctors and lawyers are broke because they never learned this simple secret. Did you ever wonder how a person can make millions of dollars a year and still be poor or why over 70% of the lottery winners squander their fortunes? Some of it has to do with their subconscious. They do not believe they deserve their wealth and the subconscious mind finds ways to squander it unwisely. You have to learn to control your money or your money will control you. That is why so many people live paycheck to paycheck. Thank goodness that many people's 401(k) plans come out before they receive their checks. Can you imagine if you had to save after the check was issued? Many people would just never do it or justify that they needed to spend the money. Just like any bill, you need to figure out that amount and save it. If it was taken out in taxes, I am sure you would be forced to adjust your lifestyle. So treat it like it is. The bottom line goal here is: create enough passive income to support your lifestyle. That's the game. If you can do this, you win the game. You also must somehow break the habit of raising your spending along with your income.

One of the basic things you need to know is: not all debt is bad. There is good debt and bad debt. Bad debts are things such as cars, loans for cars, boats and other depreciating items. I will tell you what I tell many people whom I have given financial advice. Life is a game of interest rates. Think about how banks make money. Grandma walks into a bank to get a 3% CD and they tell her that if she breaks her $10,000 CD she will get a penalty. So Grandma dares not break the CD. They then loan that money to Johnny who wants to buy a truck for $10,000 at 9%. The difference in the CD and truck loan is the spread that the bank makes. In this case the bank makes 6%. That is why banks want deposits. They will tell you free checking if you leave a $500 minimum balance where they pay you practically nothing. They then loan that money to Johnny at 9% and make a 9% profit. This spread is important to understand. Let's say that you have two credit cards at 18% and a credit card at 9%. Which one will you pay off first? Easy right! The 18%. I just told a client who wanted to invest $100,000 that I would not do so unless he uses $60,000 of those monies to pay off his credit cards at $18-21%. However, as simple as that question is, people come to me all the time asking if they should pay off the mortgage at 6%? I ask them the same question. Why are you taking the money out of something paying 8% to pay off a 6% loan that is tax deductible, which technically puts that rate lower than the 6%?

This brings up the story of my father. My dad who was 70 and owns a house here in Pennsylvania worth about $200,000 said to me that the winters were getting tough, and he wanted to move to a warmer climate in South Carolina, plus he loves to golf! I said, "Dad, you are going to take a 30 year mortgage at $120,000." He said, "Oh my goodness, I will be close to a 100 years old and the house will still not be paid for. (By the way banks cannot discriminate against age.) Why would I do such a thing?" I told my dad that the key was the rates of return. Today I pay my dad's mortgage of $505 and give him an extra $300 a month for golf, plus he gets a tax deduction on the interest rate. I said to my dad if there was a 40 year mortgage then his payments would be about $400 and I could give him $400 a month for things he enjoys doing like golf. He said that sounded great and asked if there is such a thing as a 100 year mortgage. I said no. The opposite of this circle is a client of mind who has 50 prime acres worth about $18 million. It has been in her family for 100 years, and she keeps bragging to me that she is a multimillionaire, and technically she is right, but she can barely put gas in her car or go out to eat. So you see it does not really matter that the house you live in is worth $10 million - unless you sell it.

Now would there be a time to pay off a mortgage, which is a good debt? Absolutely! If my dad would have told me that, "I really do not need that extra $300 a month. All I do is put it in the bank because I cannot spend all the monies that are coming in" (a good problem to have!), then you would use that lump sum that generates that income to pay off debt or that mortgage. So remember: always compare rates - especially rates that can be sustained every year. Which means your mutual fund will not cut it.

One way to achieve wealth quickly is through leveraging or using other peoples' money. You have probably done this already. How? Your home. You put down a down payment and borrowed the rest from a bank. Leverage comes not just from other people's money but from other people's time as well. We will talk about leverage when we discuss real estate, but leverage can be used with almost any investment opportunity you will come across in your lifetime.

Investing

There are just some basic things everyone should have in their lifetime while working:

1. A Will and a Living Will with power of attorney and medical directives. It is said that 85% of the population does not have a will. And most people with whom I have experience might have a will but not a living will. Everyone DOES NOT need a TRUST. I have seen so many people get scammed into getting a trust for $2,000-$3,000. I had one couple with no children and renting with limited assets put into a trust. These companies, typically from attorneys outside your area, have an advisor, who probably is not licensed, convincing you that they are going to save you all this money and probate costs, when in fact it can all be done inside your will. They then try to sell you investments - typically indexed annuities. If you cannot afford a will, there are many organizations that will help you such as findlegalhelp.org or www.abanet.org/legalservices/probono/directory.html, click on your state and you might get some free help. The American Bar Association has many pro-bono programs with aspiring law students who could help. www.freeadvice.com is another great source to help you in many areas of the law for free!

2. Savings. But savings in the right vehicles. If you want to remain poor then spend everything you have. Poor people look for immediate gratification. I am not saying to live like a pauper, but balance is necessary to get ahead in life. One of the reasons for immediate gratification is because they are unhappy about something in their life. It is a lack of fulfillment, a use of their energy through spending money. You can spend money, but spend it on assets rather than depreciating assets. We will distinguish between assets to buy, such as real estate and businesses, and depreciating assets such as clothes and cars. You want to think of a dollar as a seed that can be planted to produce more dollars.

3. Life Insurance – Whole life was originally designed to give you life insurance and have you save for retirement. But the only problem is

that the average rate on the savings part is about 2.4% - not even keeping up with inflation. More about life insurance later.

4. Retirement plans. The number one rule of savings is to put money in a retirement plan especially if your company will match you like 401(k) plans do. Do not put money in an IRA or outside investments unless you first put in what the company is matching you. Why? Because if they are matching you 50 cents on the dollar up to 6% you contribute then put in 6%. The reason being is because no one can guarantee you a 50% return. By not putting money in 6%, in this example, is like turning down an investment that will guarantee you 50%. Also, a lot of people do not know that these qualified retirement plans are excluded from bankruptcy and lawsuits. A good example of this is OJ Simpson. He was sued and lost a civil case filed against him by the Goldmans. He lost assets, but they could not touch his retirement plans. That is how he is able to maintain his lifestyle. (You do not see endorsement deals anymore, plus the Goldmans have rights to them.) The reasoning for this is because if you are stripped of everything you become another problem of the government. By the way, I have met many individuals who thought they missed out on a pension because their old company went out of business or merged. The only thing I can say if you might be one of them is to look up www.pbgc.gov/search and enter in your name, company name of where you worked to see if you might be entitled to a benefit. Also, the same thing about life insurance, which we will talk about shortly. Life insurance was a very popular product to sell to young people starting off and there have been so many mergers in this industry that many people come to me with very old policies, not sure if they are worth anything. Nowadays it is very easy, just go to www.unclaimed.org and your friends at the National Association for Unclaimed Property Administrators will let you know or the National Association of Life Insurance Companies at www.naic.org can help. Lastly to my fellow veterans. (I was A Sea Bee in the Navy after I graduated college and served in the first Persian Gulf War in 1991.) Look up www.va.gov or call 877-294-6380 about a missing pension or life insurance at 877-294-6380. They will tell you what you need to have when you call, probably your DD-214, but everything can be obtained for free through the Internet or by writing.

5. IRA/Roth IRA. A sad statistic is that less than 10% of individuals who are eligible to contribute to an IRA do so. Very sad. You can contribute

to an IRA if your income is at or below $166,000 for a couple and $105,000 for an individual. Or if you do not participate in or your employer does not offer a formal/qualified retirement plan, then it does not make a difference what your income is. Also IRA's are excluded from bankruptcies and lawsuits up to a million dollars. When I ask people what their investment is in an IRA, they say it is the IRA. When you think of an IRA, I want you to think of an umbrella. That is all it is, it means that it shelters you from the rain, which in this case is the taxes. It is up to you or the advisor to choose the investment vehicle. Here is a short list of vehicles: Mutual Funds, CD's, stocks, annuities, individual bonds, real estate, etc. Not a valuable car. The simple difference between a traditional IRA and a Roth IRA is that the traditional is tax deductible upfront but the Roth is not. Roth is tax free at the end while the traditional is taxable. Both grow tax deferred. What should you choose between Roth or a Traditional IRA? A lot depends on what income tax bracket you will be in when you retire. Now I know it is hard to predict, but if you can see how many years of compounding you will have using a predictable interest rate, also how many years you can conservatively put away, with a financial calculator you can see the amount you will have at retirement. I truly believe that everything that you own should not be in a traditional IRA because it could affect your tax bracket if you need a lump sum of money instead of just an income stream. With a Roth, you can make a one-time $10,000 free withdrawal before the age of 59 ½ FOR A FIRST TIME HOME BUYER. First time does not mean that you never bought a home before, it means that over the last two years you did not own a home, however you can only use this once.

6. College savings. I really believe the best way to save for college is through the 529 plans. They can be excluded from the annual gift tax where you could pay up to $65,000 a year in a gift instead of the standard $13,000 a year. They are also tax deferred and, if used for college, tax free. Also, something that is extremely important is that it is probably the only thing you can save for college and have CONTROL of. So if Johnny is partying and does not go to class, you can pass the monies to another sibling or wait until Johnny finally matures. Lastly it can be excluded from financial aid, grants and scholarships if it is with a parent instead of in the student's name because the parent has control over the asset. So, that means that the student/child has to be careful that they trust you/the parents because you are able to change

the beneficiary anytime you want. If the assets are in the student's name that is counted toward financial aid, scholarships, etc. 529's do not cover room and board and transportation, but pretty much everything else. Websites like collegeboard.com can help with planning to help with comparing financial aid packages and costs. The Coverdale could be good as well but you could only save $2,000 a year. The Roth IRA is not counted in the financial aid package when calculating what is needed out of your pocket. What is great about the 529 plans is that they have age-based investment programs that diversify the portfolio based on the child's age. If you are saving for your child's college through CD's or savings bonds, you are missing most of the benefits of the 529 plan and you have to save probably twice as much because the rate of return is much lower than what you could probably earn on a 529 plan. ONE HUGE side note: The worst thing you can do is pay for your child's college and then later become a financial burden to them later on in life. You can always borrow for college but you cannot borrow for retirement. That is why you max your 401k, 403b, 457 etc. especially if the company is matching you - then max out your IRA. Save for college and do it when they are first born. Lastly, there are so many unclaimed scholarships. Please call up and check with your local Rotary, Lions, and Legion clubs. You can buy some of these lists online. You will be shocked about how much money you can raise and everything counts. Please, parents do not sacrifice your retirement for college planning. You just become a problem to your child later on in life.

- Be careful with any prepaid stuff like college or funeral expenses. What you are really doing if you think about it is getting a rate of return that is equal to inflation; you are simply avoiding price increases. So if funeral expenses go up at an annual increase of 3% then you average a three percent return. If instead you would have taken that lump sum and invested in a rate of return of say at least 6%, you would be able to pay for two funerals instead of just one. College, by the way, has an inflation rate of about 7%.

7. Health Insurance. Very important and it goes up three times the rate of inflation. The number one cause for bankruptcy in America is health costs with credit cards coming in second. MSA is a great tool if you are self-employed. What it does is you save to pay some taxes and pay medical benefits like an IRA. Also you can carry over the bal-

ance from one year to the next. You can also have greater control over your health care dollars along with some tax benefits and perhaps even lower monthly premiums. Mention this to your health care professional, it could be worth taking a look at.

8. Social Security. The average benefit is over $13,000. It was supposed to be a supplement for the minority but has turned into the main source of income in retirement for most Americans. In fact, 1/3 of our population relies on Social Security alone while 2/3 would be in poverty without it. In 2017 Social Security will be paying out more than what it takes in so reserves will come into play. When President Franklin D Roosevelt wanted to find out what age is optimal for social security, he went to Germany to find out the typical life expectancy and then set the social security benefit at that age. The reason why is that he really did not want to have people rely on the benefit. Also true, but sad, is what were you supposed to do before you receive it... That's right - die. However, the good and bad news is that we are living longer. So what you have been seeing is that Congress continues to make the age you collect social security older. The benefit is based on 35 years of employment. As a rule they always collect social security early unless you are working, because the years that you missed compounded by a rate of return is slightly similar. Also, if you die, your spouse will get either her or your social security benefits, whichever is higher. Remember that if you are over 50 and disabled and taking care of a child, you can collect earlier.

9. One goal to any investing strategy is to learn to pay yourself first. The first 10% goes to you. I wish I was the government, I would force everyone who earns a paycheck or profits have to take 10% and invest for the long term in a passive investment like a Growth and Income mutual fund. The wealth in this country would be tremendous. The second key is to spend less than what you earned. For most Americans, this is all they have to do.

You do not want to spend money out of your IRA. A good strategy could be this: Take a lump sum of less, say $500,000, out of your IRA and pay the taxes of $200,000. Take the monies and gift it over to an Irrevocable Life Insurance Trust (ILIT). The ILIT purchases life insurance, specifically a second-to-die policy on you and your spouse. Depending on your health, age, and other factors this could generate a death benefit of $1 million to $3 million dollars. The great thing about life insurance is that it passes along tax free to the trust. Depending if the laws change, the proceeds could possibly be estate tax free to your children, rather than having a million dollar IRA be fully taxable and probably have less money than you could get out of the life insurance policy. Use the simple formula of the rule of 72. If you divide 72 by an interest rate of 7%, it would take 10.28 years to double, and then your children will pay taxes while the life insurance is tax free. Also it continues to grow.

If you do not want to pay taxes on your IRA, you could buy life insurance on your own life inside of your IRA and pay no taxes initially. When you die, the life insurance company pays a life insurance death benefit to your IRA. You will build up cash value that would still be taxable, but the life insurance will be tax free to your spouse. Take into consideration taxes that your spouse would have to pay on the IRA, and many times this could give you a better benefit than the taxes you would have to pay on a normal IRA. Remember the bottom line is how much money after taxes is actually passed to your beneficiary after the government gets its cut.

By the way, one last comment on taxes: for people who are retired, I see that many do not bother to file a tax return because their income is very low. Mistake – typically their withholding may entitle them to a refund as long as they amend their returns within three years. Always file a return. If you have parents who do this, make sure they file next year. They will be thanking you when they get some money back from Uncle Sam!

If you think I am kidding, there was over $1 billion owed to people last year who did not file a return. Also, if you moved, make sure you contact the IRS at 800-829-1040 to get your check.

So, your goal is to max out your retirement plan at work, utilize your life insurance investment vehicles, then your IRA. After you do this, then you go to investments outside these areas unless you are saving for your children's college fund.

For most people, the 529 plan for college is the best plan. Why? It is excluded from the annual gift tax, in which you can put up to $65,000 in a lump sum rather than just $13,000 a year. Also, it is the only plan you can have control of - which means if Johnny wants to use the money to buy a Jacuzzi for his frat brothers, you can say no and wait until he matures to use the college money. Other plans such as Coverdell you can only put in $2,000, he/she has to use the money by age 30 or they will receive a 10% penalty and exchanging it to another person is complicated. It grows tax deferred and if used for college it is tax free! (Similar to a Roth IRA)

Lastly, if the 529 is in the parents' name, for example, it could be excluded from financial aid, grants and scholarships. Why? Because it comes down to who has control over the money. If it's the grandparents, then they can change the beneficiary of the college money anytime they want. (You better trust your parents). Because of the exclusion from the annual gift tax, grants, scholarships and if you add in the tax deferred and tax free benefits, it is hard to beat the 529 plan for college.

Remember that the government acts in selfish ways. They want you to own a house because if you cannot provide yourself a home, it can cost the government, i.e. housing projects. They want you to own a business because if everyone was looking for a job, then we would all be unemployed. They want you to own your own business and become successful because if you are, you create jobs. They want you to save for retirement because if you do not, then you have to rely on social security and other government programs. Social security was meant to be a supplement for the few but has turned into an entitlement program for the majority. This has thus turned into a major problem for us. So the government only gives you a few ways of savings in a tax favorable manner. Therefore, your goal is to max out your retirement plan at work, especially up to what they match and then max out your personal IRA accounts called either an IRA or a Roth IRA. There are limits to allowing you to max out the personal accounts. One limit has to do with whether you are participating in a company retirement plan and the other has to do with your income, which as I write this is $95,000-$115,000 married or $59,000-$69,000 if single. Another comment about your retirement plan is that it comes out in pre-tax dollars and most of the time taken out of your plan automatically. Thank goodness for this because if individuals would have to write the check, I would guarantee you that participation levels would fall down significantly as stated earlier.

It is statistically written that people spend more time planning a vacation than they do planning their retirement. One last benefit - by contributing on a monthly basis, you are dollar cost averaging. Dollar cost averaging is buying a certain dollar amount of an investment on a regular scheduled basis regardless of the fluctuation in the price of the security. You buy more shares when prices are low and less when prices are high. For example, you want to save a $100 a month. In January, you bought $1 so you bought 100 shares. In February, you bought 118 units when the price fell down to 85 cents. In March when it rose to 95 cents you purchased 105 units and in April when the price went up to $1.05 a share you bought only 95 units. In the end you bought 418 units at an average cost of 96 cents with an investment worth $439 in four months.

You see, there are things that the government will give you, and it is all for the government's purposes.

THERE ARE SO MANY PEOPLE who do not understand what diversification really is. They come into my office and say they have done fundamental or technical analysis on their 25 different funds or 30 stocks. After their long explanations, I tell them that they are not diversified, and they say, "What are you talking about?" I mention that they are all just equities. That is why, for most people, having all your money with a money manager is a rip off. I will tell you why. There could be some variation of different types of investment vehicles, but it is all equities.

So, if the Dow in general moves up or down, you can be sure that your investments will do the same, plus they charge you one percent. Where is the discount when they lose you money? It is basically a way for the advisor to annuitize his business and make it more valuable with dependable income that comes in each quarter. They wake up January 1st and know they have income coming in and do not have the stress of finding as much new business as without it. In the long run, it is very expensive. I would bet 75% of all people who are the buy-and-hold type of investors would do better without. If investing with a money manager or owning all mutual funds and stocks is not the answer, then what is? I can tell you it is not having all your assets in CD's or cash, or worse yet trying to time the market. That is why since 1936 to 2013 if you would have just kept your assets in the S&P500, you would have averaged 10.33% compared to the average investor who only averaged 3.8%. Why? They tried to time the market. Also, since most investors do not understand the basics of investments, because they did not take courses in college or high school, they do not understand even the basics of investments. The scary thing is that companies in the future will have more defined contribution plans, such as 401(k)s, instead of pension plans thus giving the investor control. And, as we all know, humans are emotional and do not like to lose money. So, they make decisions based off of emotions rather than facts.

Thus, what is diversification? It is owning different direct asset classes. Let me give you some examples:

Individual bonds NOT bond funds. When interest rates go up and down, your rate and principal can lose money in mutual funds while this can be a different in an individual bond. In an individual bond, your interest rate is fixed and it is based off the par value of the bond and as long as you hold onto the bond then it does not make a difference what the value of the bond is. Let me tell you my famous bond story...

Owning an individual bond is like me loaning you a cow. Here are the terms. I am going to loan you my cow and all you are required to do is give me 7 gallons of milk a day. Return my cow back to me at 10,000 lbs which was the same weight I gave her to you. We agree. You work the cow hard and it is the winter when grass is not that plentiful, so she loses weight. I do not care as long as you give me my 7 gallons a milk a day and return my cow back to me at 10,000 lbs. Now let's say it is the summer time and the cow is eating a lot and weighs 14,000 lbs. Are you required to give me more milk? No, just the 7 gallons of milk a day. The good thing for me is that I can go back to you when she weighs 14,000 pounds and say I do not want the cow for the milk, but for the meat. There have been many times when we took the interest when the value was lower because we were using the bond for income only to sell the bond for 20-30% profits a few years later, when interest rates fell dramatically and when mutual funds were down 30%+.

ICON. A lease company. When companies default, the stocks starts to fall, then they start to default on preferred stock holders, then bond holders. So, even if they default on all of these investments it does not mean they default on their leases. A good example of this is Kmart, which went bankrupt, so if you owned the previous three asset classes you would have lost money, but they never missed a lease payment. Why? Because they needed the leased equipment to operate and work their way out of bankruptcy. Have you ever noticed that some airlines in the past went bankrupt but they never cancelled your flight. Why? They need that airplane to work their way out of bankruptcy. The equipment they lease is critical for the company to operate. Coke cannot get their products delivered without the use of trucks. The assets they use, airplanes, trucks, ships, manufacturing equipment, are critically important for the operation of the business. Some companies like this to consider are Home Depot, NBC, Wal-Mart, Coca-Cola, Nabisco, and Whirlpool. Enron was a company that never missed a lease payment. Why? Though people saw the company stock start to plummet, they did not miss a lease payment since people out West still needed energy. So, they leased the equipment to someone else. For ICON, I doubt that all these large companies that comprise the investment lease pool go, not bankrupt, but non-existent at the same time! In 2008, while your stocks were getting crushed, ICON paid out 9%+. You see this is a private company not affected by interest rates or the market. And all investments are typically affected by either interest rates or the market.

Let's talk about that for a moment. Investing is really kind of simple. It is the number of choices that confuses us. You can either choose a fixed investment such as CD's, government or corporate bonds, fixed annuities, money markets, etc. or variable investments such as mutual funds, stocks, UIT's, variable annuities, public REITs, etc. When interest rates go up or down, they affect the fixed side. When the market goes up or down, they affect the variable side. What you need are assets that are not affected by either to such a large degree. ICON is such a product. Private LP's are such a product.

Another example of this is INLAND. Inland has been in business since 1967, has done over 405 investment programs, and as I write this, never lost one penny for their investors. They have over 300 million dollars in cash, and; was 2009 a great time for buying real estate? It sure was. Inland was buying properties at 20-30% discounts and interest rates are close to all-time lows in the history of monitoring rates. We always want to buy low and sell high, and the people who do not understand that this is a great time to buy just will never get it. When should you buy a home in Florida? Do you buy the home in the fall, winter, spring, or summer? The summer, of course, because that is when the snow birds return home and there are fewer buyers. Also, when they lease their buildings, they are leasing them to a majority of large companies, AT&T headquarters, 39% of all the Wal-Mart's, 41% of all the Target stores, the University of Pennsylvania signed a long lease. These are large institutions and they are typically done for 20 years. Think about yourself. You might default on you credit cards but you would never think about defaulting on your home.

Also remember that this is a PRIVATE LP. In 2008, during one of the last markets since the Great Depression, you would have made a 602% return. This is another example of a non-correlated asset.

Is owning real estate in a mutual fund the same thing? NO. Anything, be it bond, real state, etc., if it has the word "fund" next to it means that it will react closely to what the market is doing.

Annuities: OK, first evaporate the negativity you have heard about this asset class. A lot of the propaganda put out by mutual funds about annuities is wrong. I have never sold a fixed annuity and probably never will. Variable annuities need to contain the Guaranteed Minimum Income or Withdrawal Benefit. The account also has the ability to lock in gains yearly and sometimes even quarterly. What these riders do is that regardless of what the stock market does, they give you income you can rely on for withdrawing money or a growth rate based on your original principal. For example, let's say that you had $250,000 to invest in September 30, 1994. You would have had over $844,000 at one point. The markets declined starting in 2000 and you wanted to retire on 9-30-2003 when your market value of your account is worth $421,747. What would you have done? In a mutual fund, there is nothing you can do because there are no guarantees. Also let's say it did come back, what happened in 2008? You would have erased most of the gains you would have received the last five years. Also, if you are withdrawing an income, let's say 4%, you would have compounded the problem even worse. With this example, in 9-30-2003, you could have annuitized/created a pension, with the investments at $844,647. Thus you would have created an income stream for the next 20 years and received $1,072,360 back. These products would have served you well in the bear market of 2008 where your income would have grown at 5% regardless of where the markets were going.

BE CAREFUL if you are invited to a seminar on trusts from a lawyer who is outside your area, and the person is trying to sell you an indexed annuity. Many people selling these indexed annuities are not even licensed, but they call themselves financial advisors. An indexed annuity will not pay you anything in a declining market - 0%, but will set a limit on how much you can make in an up market. This is typically 8%. They typically have long times where you cannot take out money without a significant penalty and high commissions. (10 years or longer)

Oil/Gas. Not through a fund but actually owning oil wells and perhaps natural gas (which will be more important in the future for the US), through a limited partnership is a good asset class to have as well. They can provide tax deductions against ordinary or passive income if you are a general partner of up to 80% or more of the original investment. However, NEVER, invest in an oil/gas investment for tax deductions alone. You must consider the returns. Some good companies will average close to a 10% return or more.

Here is the BIG POINT that I really want you to get. The key to diversification is owning different asset classes. How about gold and silver, direct oil and gas LP's, etc.? Let's say you have a lump sum of money and do not know what to do. So you would have listened to my advice and put 20% in individual bonds, 20% in ICON, 20% in Inland, 20% in the VA annuity with a guarantee attached to it, and the remaining 20% in mutual funds and stocks. Let's assume the market went down 30%. Did you lose any monies in the bonds? No, not for the income you are receiving. ICON – No, Inland – No, the VA? Not with the rider which grows regardless of what the market does. Mutual funds and stocks - probably. So in this situation you have 80% of your assets that made money. Now does that prevent you from having growth? No, you would have had growth in the mutual funds, the VA, and Inland (which has potential for growth besides the dividend that they provide). While ICON and typically the bonds would have no growth potential. (Think of the bonds like a cow, even though they do have growth potential through the meat as in my prior example.) So, when the markets did do well, we still had 60% of these investments that have growth potential. This is what is meant by diversification - different asset classes. With gold and silver, direct buying has been very hot lately, but it is like a trend. If you look at gold over the last 50 years, its average return is only 4.4%.

MUTUAL FUNDS – HERE IS A BIG POINT AND I MEAN BIG POINT. No one knows which is the best stock to pick. Unless they have a crystal ball, they are all just guessing and mostly guessing wrong. What is the difference between Fidelity, Vanguard and T. Rowe Price? Nothing. I have included in the back of this book statistics that show that money managers could be right and outperform the market for a few years only to underperform the markets in later years. When averaged, returns with money managers actually have made less than if you owned all markets across the world. They advertise so much and have so much money that they have been hiding this secret for many years. Also they keep the magazines in business by advertising in them so they hide the secret as well. Think about it. Each month they need to have a different headline to catch your attention. They cannot keep the same headline on investing or the magazine would be out of business. These firms want to trick you into believing that they have the answer. If they had an individual who could do that then we would all invest with that fund or individual. But they do not. Also consider the cost. There are so many hidden costs such as the set up cost and the market maker who could have a percentage cost of up to 6%. How would you like for me to take away a 6% return every year from your fund performance?

If you believe that the track record of a money manager is the key – you will be disappointed. If you believe in market timing, and you pretend to have a crystal ball that predicts the future – you will be disappointed. If you think you know the future of a company or a stock – you will be disappointed. So, what do you do, especially since in the future, pensions will go away, and we will be left with only 401(k)'s... Let's consider, what is a 401(k)? It is simply a choice of mutual funds or company stock.

So, what do you do? What is the truth? It is what Dr. Harry Markowitz, Nobel Prize winner and Eugene Fama developed. Basically, you want to pick a portfolio across the efficient frontier. Use correlation and take into consideration the market factor, the size factor, and the value factor. Own all asset classes which actually bring down the risk of the portfolio. Add together the Modern Portfolio Theory and the Three Factor Model and you have a free market portfolio.

OK, I PROBABLY WENT OVER YOUR HEAD. Here is what you do, simply in layman's terms; look up online 'Matson Money' – this is the firm that brought this to our attention. They will find you a coach, not a sales person or a financial advisor or even a CERTIFIED FINANCIAL PLANNER™ who is not trained to be a coach. They will educate you and do it for free through seminars or events. Please understand that if this secret gets out that it will devastate the mutual fund companies. But it will finally bring the truth to the public and stop the frustrations of getting let down by another fund or money manager that think they have the answer and could magically predict the future. Boy, what a change it would be.

Unfortunately, we are not taught about investments in school, are bored about investments, or have a hard time understanding investments so most people do not seek the truth. If you are reading this you know it and will wonder why everyone is not doing this. Through time and word of mouth, the general public will get rid of the disappointment the mutual fund companies have created. However, there will be a fight because these companies, and magazines too have lots of money, and the media will try their hardest to stop us. But in all honesty, this is the only way of owning equities; it is scientifically proven and will help you create a portfolio that will give you returns that are justified by the risk you take.

I know that you might not have a choice because these large firms have been offering services for employers to provide their 401(k)'s. But you will know that when you roll your money to an IRA. You will have a better choice than trusting a money manager who is educated but still speculating and gambling with your money without really knowing what is going to happen in the future. Trust me, what I told you is big news but will take some coaching to truly have an understanding. What you need to know by reading this book is that funds do not matter, money managers do not know, and you must diversify through different asset classes through alternative investments. I could write a whole book on this subject myself.

There are no magic investments. If there were then most advisors would be wealthy instead of broke. That is why they call themselves brokers. (Just having a little fun.) This brings up one last subject: how advisors get paid and from where you should be getting your advice...

The school systems have done a great job educating us on the hierarchy of knowledge. The same is true of authority in the military. For example, in education, you have the Ph.D., then Master's, then the Bachelor's, then a high school diploma, and lastly no high school diploma. With finances though, everyone giving advice seems to be on the same playing field, and people do not know where to get advice. The independent CERTIFIED FINANCIAL PLANNER I believe is the best.

The CFP® will become the designation like what the CPA is to accounting, one day. Independent? Why? Because the advisor is not forced to sell you a product because a company is pushing it. Also, they have products that most broker/dealers will not even offer. Try getting ICON, Carter Validus, FSI or Oil/GAS deals as mentioned above at these firms, good luck! The bottom line is that you at least want an advisor who has a certain level of knowledge and who is acting in your best interest and not mandated to sell you a particular product to satisfy his branch manager.

Next would be the wirehouses. Good luck with less than $250,000. Even above this amount, selling proprietary and limited products for the company's own interest is not the way to go. Even if they say they do not do this, why take a chance if there is even some type of temptation that this could be the case.

Banks: Most advisors sit behind the desk having clients come to them. Same thing as the wirehouse - the banks got into the business because they wanted an extra stream of income and saw how much money the wirehouses were making and wanted to have some of that revenue.

Life insurance companies: They mask themselves as wirehouses, but many insurance advisors have their Series 6 license, so they sell you variable annuities and mutual funds because those are the asset classes you can sell with a Series 6 license. The worst of all are the people selling these indexed annuities. Since these are considered fixed income products, the advisors do not have to have a securities license. A lot of these advisors hook up with an out of state law firm to sell trusts to people who would be better off with a simple will, at four times less the cost. As far as I am concerned, these individuals are the slime of the industry. Just remember to make sure your advisor is independent and a CFP®. One last note, many people do not send in those pieces of paper when there is a class action lawsuit against a company. It is worth filling out for a few minutes of your time even if it is for $100. Now we do not know what the amount will be, but you get my point.

How advisors get paid. The big thing today is having managed accounts for a fee of less than, say, 1% with a "money manager." The question that should be asked is where is my discount for losing me money in 2008? They get paid no matter what, and if they say, "well we did not make as much money because your account is down," that is almost laughable. What happens is that they do not charge you any commissions for buying or selling, but just a flat 1%. From a monetary standpoint of the advisor and the firm, this is how they make the most money over the long run. It is a way for the advisor to annuitize his business to have recurring revenue flow through the door without getting new business. Think about it, what is 1% of 200,000 million dollars in assets under management? Nice revenue and all you have to do is maintain the relationship with the client. Fee based accounts can be very expensive and you will think twice about asking for advice because you know it is going to cost you. This advice at least takes the bias out of the advisor selling you something for the commission.

Commissioned accounts - probably still right for most people - especially if you are a buy-and-hold type of investor. Just remember some basic things such as, in most situations, class A shares on mutual funds for the long term is typically the best and for the short term it is the C share. That is when an advisor is continuously buying and selling, he is doing so most likely for commissions and it is actually illegal. This is called "churning". No load means no commissions, but also no help, and for the majority of our population which has little to no knowledge of investing, that's not the way to go. A good example is the people who chase after the returns picking the latest funds in *Money Magazine*. Here is a great example: in February 1992, the front cover of Money magazine stated "20 great mutual funds to buy now". So you bought them. Then in February 1993, it was "The 12 funds to buy now". So you bought them. One fund is mentioned again this year, you now own 31 funds. February 1994, "The nine funds to buy now". None of the 31 funds are mentioned this year. You now own 40 mutual funds. February 1995, "Eight most dependable funds". None of the previously mentioned funds are mentioned again this time. You now own 48 different mutual funds. December 1995 "The one that beats them all". This fund has not been mentioned once in the prior 4 years. Now you own 49 mutual funds.

So to recap, while working, you should have a will and a living will, life insurance for either spouse to replace income. And for estate planning purposes or investment purposes. Max out your retirement plan at work at least up to the match preferably maxing it out. Then max out your IRA if you meet the requirements. Then lastly, provide funding for your child's college plan through a 529 plan. How about after retirement? Then it is called the Big Three:

1. Estate planning. What this basically means is that whoever is supposed to get the assets gets them and we avoid the government killing us through taxes. Once you have a certain net worth, the government then taxes you so that they can distribute the wealth to others in greater need, at least that's the concept. The reason for this is so that certain families do not retain all the wealth and possibly control society as a whole, thus creating the temptation of abuse. There are some techniques that can help you in this area. First, think of the government giving you a coupon worth a certain dollar amount. The government will give this coupon to a wife and husband. Now, when one spouse dies then they take away this coupon. These coupons are important because of a thing called "estate tax" which means as I write this anything over $5.12 million amount can be taxed as high as tax rates of 35%. To avoid the government taking away this coupon, you have to create a trust so that the coupon goes to the trust rather than being taken away. Typically, as part of this trust you are allowed to take income for your normal living expenses but spending it in a lump sum is usually prohibited, and if you do so the government might say that is in violation of law and take away this coupon. You do not have to worry about having a trust set up if your net worth is not over a certain dollar amount. There are certain exceptions such as having a

special needs trust child. Many times a special needs adult will need to be supervised so that certain individuals will not take advantage of them. For second marriages a QTIP trust is many time necessary. A QTIP trust is a Qualified terminable interest Property. This is a very complex area and there are so many good things that you can do from family limited partnerships to dynasty trusts. One other hint about attorneys: there are too many who try to be everything to everyone. Lastly, do not forget about a stretch IRA. When we pass our IRA's to our loved ones, our loved ones have to pay taxes on the lump sum with, starting December 31st the following year of receiving it, or the 5 year rule applies. (Consult with a tax professional. Now, to have control and lessen the tax burden, we are allowed to "stretch" the IRA for two generations. What this means is that our children can draw an income from it and then it passes to our second generation or our grandchildren. Then it has to be taken as a lump sum. If not, the Rockefellers would have done this in perpetuity and created a dynasty. Please make sure you hire an attorney who specializes in estate planning. Another warning in estate planning is to have liquid assets available for your beneficiary for the "death tax" because taxes are due within nine months from date of death. This can cause an issue. I had a client who had lots of real estate but virtually no liquid cash. We had to liquidate some of his buildings with steep discounts to satisfy the taxes.

2. LTC – Long Term Care. Everyone automatically thinks nursing home. How wrong could you be; most of your care will be spent in your home. Then the second step is an assisted living facility or adult day care, then lastly a nursing home. If I could avoid paying insurance on most things, I would. The reason being is because statistically you are paying for something you will not collect on and the insurance companies make billions because of this. Now thank goodness for insurance companies, I want them to be profitable, because they serve a huge purpose. However, I am not the one who would like to over-contribute to their profits. So, I would only like to insure the things that I probably will collect on. Statistically the odds of using long term care for a couple is over 50%, unlike having our houses burn down which is 1/1200, or totaling your car in an accident which is 1/800. So when you see those types of odds, you better protect against it.

3. As a matter of fact, the number one issue in America is not the social security system going broke, it is the Medicare/Medicaid system. It is

only going to get worse because the majority of our population is getting older. These days I see people all the time who want to gift their assets to their children to avoid the government and nursing homes collecting the assets, but there is a five year look back period that the government can go back and take those assets from your children. I hear it is expensive; well, that's because people wait until they are seventy and have health issues.

4. The key to getting long term care at a reasonable price is to get the coverage when you are in your mid to early sixties and are reasonably healthy. Also, if you are self-employed, it could be tax deductible. Long term care is not right for everyone, especially if you do not have many assets to protect and paying the premiums will change your lifestyle.

5. Investments. Which we just discussed above. When you retire, you draw an income from all your sources to provide you with your standard of living. From Social Security, pensions, rental property, retirement plans, businesses, and/or savings.

Anyone can truly be rich with discipline but it is nice to have a high paying job that will get you there sooner because you can save more. Let me give you an example. John is 30 years old and wants to retire at 60 so he puts away the max in his 401(k) plan of $15,500 a year and his company matches him 30%, so they put in $4,650 as a match. His wife, Mary, does not have an IRA, so she puts in the max of $5,000 in her IRA. They also save another $500 a month because they save some of the raises that they get at their job. Additionally, Mary received a small inheritance from her grandmother of $30,000, she spent about $10,000 on her new kitchen and put away the rest because that is what her grandmother would want her to do until they retire. Thirty years later, what do they have? On a financial calculator you input $20,000 present value, 30 years, 8% as the interest rate, the future value would be $201,253. Not bad. That would generate about $838 a month, add in Social Security between the two of them for about $3,400 a month and you have a decent lifestyle depending on inflation of about 4%.

The curse of waiting. Let's say you have a brother Fred. At the age of 25 he invested $2,000 a year for 10 years then at the age of 35 he had a nervous breakdown and could not work or did not want to work. You started investing not at 25 like your brother Fred but at the age of 35. You put away more, $3,000 a year and did it for 30 years instead of 10, like your brother Fred. Guess who has more at the end? That's right. Fred has $611,817 at the age of

64 earning 10% while you have $542,830 at the age of 65 earning 10%. If you waited until 45 to start and put away $9,000 a year for 20 years, you have $567,022 at 65, and if you were 55 and wanted to catch up and saved $30,000 a year for 10 years, you would have $525,935 at age 65. Einstein said that one of the wonders of the world should be compounding of interest. Like he was on many things, I think he was right.

Some other common mistakes…

Moving assets to cash or other ultra-conservative investments. Especially if you are trying to gain back some of your losses. If you are down 50%, how much do you need to get back your losses? The answer is 100%. How about down 35%? Now you have to make up 55%, how about 40%? 50% or 60%? 150%. People do this because of emotions. But history is a great teacher because it tends to repeat itself. In 1972, if you had a $100,000 by mid-year in 1974 you would have had only about $57,000 left. I am sure most people would say I had enough of this and would have bailed for the rest of their lives into conservative investments. Mistake - because that same investment kept in the S&P 500 would have grown back to about $245,000 in 10 years while your CD at 5% would only be worth $93,429.

Bottom line here is: Diversification in different assets class is the key. Also remember that when the market advances through a trough, it typically advances 16.4% after 3 months, 22.65% after 6 months and 37.1% after one year. The key is to buy low and sell high, right? Well, at the beginning of 2009 that is what buying low felt like. Remember that EVERY investment holds risk. Even a CD has inflation risk and sometimes liquidity risk, too.

Not taking money out when you turn 70 ½: this is called Required Minimum Distribution. If you do not take out the money that the government requires you to take out, then you are taxed at 50%. How much you have to take out depends on the IRS tables. Also you do not have to take out the money from every IRA, it could be taken out from just one IRA as long as it is enough from the sum of all IRAs.

Thinking that your pension is backed by the government and Pension Benefit Guaranty Corp.? The maximum benefit they will pay is $55,840.92 as of 2013. I have met clients who worked for Delta and U.S Airways who received less than 70% of what they were promised. Plus the PGBC is in serious debt, over $10 billion over its long term obligations. By the way, I have been around numerous people whose companies have been out of business thinking they do not have any pension. (Go to www.pbgc.gov and look for missing participants and see if you could find that missing pension.)

Not taking into consideration the biggest enemy for a retiree – inflation! An easy way to explain this is to ask an elder what they paid for their first house.

My parents paid $30,000. Today, that is the cost of a car. With just a 3% inflation rate, with an income of $50,000, you would need $67,196 in 10 years, $90,306 in 20 years and $140,963 in 35 years. How about 5% of that $50,000 you are receiving, you would need that to be $81,445 in ten years, $132,665 in 20 years and $275,801 in 35 years. How about 7%? You might be thinking there is no way inflation would average this high again. I beg to differ, especially with all the cash that has been pumped into the economy by the government recently. At 7% with $50,000 you would need $98,358 in ten years, $193,484 in 20 years and $533,829 in 35 years. You also might be thinking 35 years is a very long time in retirement, but let's look at some stats. A male at 65 has a 49% chance of living to 86 and a 26% chance of living to 92. A female who is 65 has a 49% chance of living to 89 and a 23% chance of living to 95. More impressive is a married couple at 65. There is a 63% chance living to 90 and a 36% chance to live to 95. The most amazing statistic is that a child born in 2009 has a 50% chance of living to over 100! So could it be possible that if you retired at 60, you might live 35 years? Yes, it is possible, especially over time with improvements in medicine. True safety deals with keeping your principal ahead of inflation and that is through a diversified portfolio with investments that have potential for large returns such as oil exploration and alternative investments with a rate over inflation. Remember our goal is becoming rich, not just getting by.

Taking Out Too Much Money During Retirement

A sustainable withdrawal rate is about 4% in mutual funds or 6% with a diversified portfolio as we discussed earlier, max. So you might think that having a million dollars is a lot of money. Not really because it only gives you $40,000 to $60,000 in income.

How the market reacts when you take out your money is extremely important. Let me give you an example. You take two investors and one has $250,000 and wants to withdraw 5% of his portfolio every year and adjust it for inflation of 3% ever year. He averages a rate of return of 7% a year for the next 30 years in retirement. If he was to get off to a bad start and had his first 3 years in retirement in a bear market with losses of -17.6%, -12.8%, and -3.5% respectively, he/she would have run out of money at the age of 79 or 17 years. If, however, lucky Bill invested the same $25,000 and averaged the same return of 7% but had those 3 bad years at the end instead of the beginning of retirement, it would last until the age of 91 and have $712,574 left over.

So, what do we do? We cannot determine what the market is going to do when we retire. This is why different asset classes are necessary, especially investments that are not related to the markets or have downside protection from the markets.

"Everything is different this time and the world is not the same." These people are not optimistic, and I would bet 95% of them are not rich and never took a chance in life. They are negative thinkers and see the glass half empty instead of half full. Ignore them, stay away from them, and if you are one, change your way of thinking with some of the techniques you have learned in this book so you can become rich. Here are some examples of how to make this happen: visualize, meditate, affirmations, reading positive books, and hang around positive people.

Here are some examples of how to FAIL:

Not paying yourself first - You should always strive to pay yourself first especially in IRA's and 401(k)'s, which could be excluded from bankruptcy and lawsuits.

Trying to do investments yourself – BIG mistake. I am an advisor, and I can tell you I could not manage my own portfolio without help. This is really the penny wise, dollar foolish mentality. You cannot be an expert in everything. It makes me laugh when people say their accountant is also their financial advisor. Why not make him your doctor as well? That is why lawyers and doctors have different disciplines and specialize in different areas. Let me tell you a secret: the wealthy individual does not do it himself. I am talking about people with a net worth of over 20 million. If you are thinking they have to handle everything themselves with that much money, you have the wrong thought process. They stick to what they know best and always use leverage. If you are taking time to learn an online trading gimmick, you are wasting your time. And trust me if you were that good, you would make tens of millions of dollars a year as a money manager. How many people have achieved this by doing it themselves? One out of a million. Perhaps you could be comfortable and do pretty well, but I will tell you that if you are doing it yourself, you are not part of the wealthy affluent and certainly not acting like a future one.

It is a CERTIFIED FINANCIAL PLANNER ™ that coordinates the big picture of taxes and estate planning and investments and organizes the information; NOT the accountant or attorney because their disciplines do not require them to do so. As a CERTIFIED FINANCIAL PLANNER ™ it is required for us to know other disciplines to some degree and organize all areas of financial planning including insurance, taxes, and the law. They might not practice these disciplines, but we are required to know aspects of these practices so we have the ability to coordinate them. If an advisor is not coordinating or meeting with your attorney or accountant, this is a sign of neglect as far as I am concerned. It would be like the surgeon who does not see the charts of the anesthesiologist or the general who does not speak with his captains on the battlefield. Well it is and if anyone thinks they can truly service their investment clients during tax season, especially if their main practice is accounting, they are being ridiculous.

Also, some people pride themselves on being with the same firm for many years. Even though loyalty is nice, it in most cases is not always the smartest practice. I am amazed that people will say things like, "I have been with Merrill Lynch for 25 years" and yet have had nine different advisors. Times change and you need to do the same as well. If you applied the same logic to medicine or technology, where would you be today? Using a typewriter and taking medicine that is not effective.

Family Member as Advisor

This happens all the time because it has to do with trust, but too many people rely too much on what Uncle Lou has to say even though he is not a professional in this area. He is limited in knowledge. It would be like asking Uncle Lou if you should have that heart operation. There is nothing wrong with asking Uncle Lou questions and then asking those questions to a professional or better yet having Uncle Lou present at the meeting with the professional...

Always get a second opinion. It is a way of clarifying questions, catching mistakes, tackling a problem from a different angle and identifying omissions.

Get rid of the mentality of trying to be perceived rich or poor. You should be more concerned about earning assets that go up in value rather than having flashy toys.

Sam Walton, one of the richest men in the world, flew first class only one time and drove an old truck and lived in a modest home. He treated money with respect. We all have been told, especially in the United States, that material possessions are the symbols of wealth. As stated before, we must first be content with what we have because if you are driven by money to satisfy your ego instead of the money working for you, you are working for it.

Putting all your money in the company stock because you work there and feel comfortable on where the company is heading

First, no diversification exists. Please use history as a lesson. ENRON is a good example. People in the company invested 60% of their retirement income in the company stock only to lose everything. Bear Stearns is another prime example and there are many others. Another reason people do this is greed. It is hard to accept 10-12% gains when their company stock is going up 40% a year.

PAY off debt. I would guess that 80% of debt is bad debt. Paying off a mortgage quicker will save most people with a $200,000 home hundreds of thousands; that's right, hundreds of thousands. If you take a 30 year mortgage at 4% for a $200,000 house it would cost you $954.83 a month. Two ways to pay off a mortgage early is to pay bi-weekly, by doing this is to make an extra payment a year. You can cut a 30 year mortgage down to 22 years. That's 8 years of payments! Let's face the fact, though, this is a pain in the butt, also some firms charge a fee to set it up this way, so try to make one extra payment a year on your own. Or you could add a little each mortgage payment directing the mortgage company to apply what you have over the minimum payment to principal instead of a payment. That is more than double what your actual house costs!! Let's face the facts, less debt means less stress, fewer fights with your spouse, and it helps take away worry and provides a sense of security. There must be one activity that if you have not done you literally need to stop and do. And that is to write down all the debt you have. Everyone equates getting out of debt by making more money but unfortunately your spending will increase with the extra amount you are making. There has to be cutbacks in spending. Just like a diet, you can exercise but if you increase your eating you will not lose weight. So first write down how much you owe and then target ONE bill at a time to pay it off. The bill with the highest rate – that is the one you concentrate on first, then use the payments after you paid off that one bill and target the next. It is really that simple, there have been books written on that subject that do not get to the bottom line which I just told you in a sentence or two. It is like a snowball, once you pay off a few bills, you gain confidence, you have momentum and paying off your bills becomes easier because you will have more money to do so. Every time you pay off a bill, celebrate! The mentality section was so necessary because getting out of debt is simple if you cut back your spending and do this technique listed above. It is like losing weight – here it is, are you ready? Eat less and move more. OK, there can be some techniques and knowing what type of foods to eat can help dramatically, but I can guarantee you that if you eat a lot less and moved around a lot more you will lose weight.

Lastly, one thing that drives me nuts is when I hear clients who are getting collection calls at 7:00 a.m. or 10:30 at night. This is against the law; they are only allowed to call between 8:00 a.m. and 9:00 p.m., that's it. More importantly, if you truly are working your way out of debt, the last thing you need is negative reinforcement, so I would recommend that you contact the companies in writing to stop contacting you and, by law, they are supposed to stop doing so. The only thing they can do is try to sue you. You still, of course, owe the debt but you will not have negative reminders in writing or through the mail.

A suggestion is to send the letter, certified mail with return receipt requested or send the letter through Fed Ex, UPS , etc. If you keep on getting letters then you can file a complaint against the company.

Not only should you know what bills you have but how much money you have as well through Social Security and pensions. Also calculate how much you will have based off your current savings. Call Social Security at 800-722-1213 and ask them to mail you a Social Security benefit statement. Also, I have clients who are taking care of older parents and had them move into their homes but never notified Social Security, thus there was money still owed to their parents. Check with Social Security when anyone in your family passes away and see if there were any benefits missing that you did not receive.

Never try to take money, in the accumulation stage of your life, out of your investments to indulge in something that is of material wealth, especially to compete against the Joneses. Give thoughtful consideration before you spend.

Always have a safety net. Three months if both spouses are working or if retired or if one spouse is working then six months. You want to be able to write a check if you have a reversal of fortune. The interest rate does not matter here. The convenience is the most important thing.

I do not know about you, but I have many clients who have savings bonds. Some as old as 35 years old in which the government actually stop paying interest on. There are billions, yes, billions of dollars of EE bonds that have never been redeemed. Mostly because clients are not aware that they had them. I advise my clients for the hell of it to go to www.savingsbonds.gov and go under a page called Treasury Hunt and enter in your information and you will see if you have any bonds that you are not aware that you even had. If you have some bonds but cannot find them, then all you have to do is fill out their form called a PDF 1048 or form PDF 3062-4 if you never got the bond. Do the same with the FDIC at www.fdic.gov for that old CD. Go to the tab "Consumer Protection" and then "Banking and Your Money" then click on the tab "Search for Unclaimed Funds." Then you download their page and mail it to the FDIC. While you are at it, check for pensions. I had a client who found an extra $375 a month by clicking on www.pbgc.gov. They even have a book for you to learn how to search for a lost pension. The last suggestion is to check with the IRS www.irs.gov. There are many people that do not file but are owed a refund.

NOT USING LIFE INSURANCE AS AN INVESTMENT. Any time you use leverage, it helps create wealth quicker and smarter. Real Estate does this and so does life insurance. Too many people do not really understand life insurance. For example if you take Bob who at the age of 30 invested $1,000 a month for 30 years and the policy earns the standard return for illustrations at

8%. The cash value would be approximately $1,512,584.40 he could then take tax free withdrawals of $360,000 tax free for the next 25 years. Thus he took out $360,000 and only invested $360,000 and the death benefit of close to $3 million would be tax free to his beneficiary. Taking into consideration taxes, insurance can be an amazing tool. I have used Equity Indexed Universal Life Policy. What is great about this investment is that it typically has lower costs than other policies, has potential for growth through the S&P 500, and the tax advantage of tax-free withdrawals because you are taking loans. Talking about leverage, a bank could help in the investment process. Rates are very favorable right now, so you could get a low rate loan and invest in an insurance policy. Especially borrowing from a home because it could be tax deductible, which lowers the actual rate of the loan taking into consideration the tax benefits. You can use the dividends to pay off the loan especially if you can get a decent return from the Equity Indexed Universal Life Policy of up to 8%. So basically the loan paid for itself by the life insurance dividends and the death benefit went to your family and it cost you nothing.

Part Three: Working for Yourself

To work for someone else is to give up freedom. You are at their mercy, and they own you to some degree – or at the very least, they own how you are spending your time. It makes you dependent. The goal in life should be self-reliance. That is why the United States rose to become the most powerful nation on Earth – PERIOD. We are governed by our self-interest. The hardest thing about working for yourself is your self-doubt. Because once you decide this is what you want, negative images will come into your mind to try to persuade you not to. But this is good, because it helps you think of hurdles that you need to overcome. However, continuously telling yourself not to think negative thoughts will make you think of negative thoughts. Of course, you know what you need to do. If not, reread the mentality section, so you can live your life to the fullest with freedom to be creative.

While being independent is the goal, we all secretly want our spouse, friends, and coworkers to take care of us, solve our problems, and make our lives easier. We were taught to be dependent on others through our childhood, so of course we want this to continue to some degree as adults. Fear, as discussed before, keeps us in this state of dependency. Real power comes from the realization that we alone are responsible for our successes and failures.

Talk to any middle school student, and they will tell you what they wish to become almost with ease: professional athletes, successful business owners, singers, etc. What happens is the harshness of rejections, which then causes us to rely on others to take care of us or the delusion that others care for us, specifically our bosses. Now, I am not saying that all bosses or employers do not care for their employees. I do myself, but never be disillusioned about the fact that we are governed by self-interest, and if need be, we will fire that individual if they do not satisfy my objectives. It sounds harsh, but it is true. If you really think about it, employers keep their employees around for our needs not for companionship. To work for someone is to give up your time, the most precious commodity that we have, in return for a relationship that is dependent on a boss who is looking out for number one. It is true that bosses want you to be dependent. We do not want you to be self-reliant because that means we will lose you and will have to find a replacement.

Anyone's goal who works for any large organization is to move higher and higher up the ladder. Why? So that you can have more freedom, where you decide the direction of the work and pursue your vision for the company. That way you do not have to depend on anyone. The fact is that if we are governed by self-interest in most situations, when bosses give you rewards, it is always with expectations that they expect something in return such as loyalty or greater effort.

Remember that every thumb print is different, which means that we are all unique. Thus it is possible for you to possess powers that others might not have. Unfortunately, not everyone believes in themselves or their unique strengths. You must not care as much as to what people think of you, and believe me, this carefree attitude attracts people to you. The bottom line is that when you work for someone else it can limit and confine you. What keeps us at these jobs that we dislike is fear, your desires to conform to what other people you know have done, and your self-doubts.

The key is to take a leap of faith and develop the mindset so that we are confident that things will indeed work out. We have thus activated our freewill that will guide us to take action. Being independent will satisfy your deepest desires for independence. This is why we spent so much time on the mentality section. It is vital that you have unwavering confidence, which will allow you to overcome obstacles that will make most people give up and quit. The most powerful force of momentum is confidence, and truly the ability to overcome anything and achieve the results we want by focusing on our own destiny.

Try to find a mentor. Of course a mentor in business and please, and this will sound like a "duh" obvious note to make, but make sure your mentor has had great success and is teaching you the same techniques he /she used to become successful. Before moving to another point, the key is to have a mentor in other areas in your life too, such as a marriage and health. A mentor does not always have to be face to face but also could be through a book, just make sure you are not getting marriage advice from someone who has been married three times.

Mentors are easy to come by. Most are willing to help and all you have to do is have the courage to ask. Just look in your community to see what people have succeeded in the area you want to achieve. Always strive to be mentored by the best even though you might fear rejection and, in your mind, do not think they will say "yes." The key to getting the mentor is to research things about that person and then think of someone that you know who might know be able to refer you. Then call or write to the person. People love to hear about themselves, so start off with things you admire about them and their success. Tell them how those qualities you admire in them could guide you into success in your own life. Then ask for a brief time perhaps each month to ask questions. (Make sure it is a brief time like 15-30 minutes max. If they volunteered more time, find and make sure you have an agenda written down each session and stop when you said that you would). Always follow up with a brief written thank you. These people truly have the keys to your success. Education does not matter, nor do looks, or English skills. Their success in life is what matters.

Try this exercise - for the next three months, speak to one millionaire per month and ask your questions. (Or feel free to keep on reading and ignore the exercise, but in reality the person who commits to this exercise has a tremendous advantage over everyone else.)

Consider where these great people started, and how far they've gone - Thomas Edison's mother was told by the headmaster that he was "retarded." Michael Landon finished almost dead last in his school and was homeless. James Gardner, seen in the movie "The Pursuit of Happiness", was homeless living in a shelter with no education or money and he became a successful businessman. We all have to start somewhere and overcome certain obstacles in our lives.

It's crucial that, when you do meet with your mentor, you don't get discouraged. Do not start comparing them to you and think of the qualities they possess and you do not have. Do not worry, one of the keys to success is to find people who have the qualities you do not possess and add them to your team.

You can learn a lot about yourself through self-psych evaluations. Then you will ultimately be aware of what your weaknesses are. If you are aware of your weaknesses, then you can hire people or work with people who have those strengths. More importantly, check your behavior when you know it is your weakness. Meaning, if you are achievement oriented, take charge, and enjoy getting results, then you are probably a poor listener, demanding, and impulsive. So, by knowing this, you might have a hard time relaxing and need to focus on listening to others and should try to be more patient. Remember, the goal to becoming successful is overcoming any hurdle, including yourself.

Anthony Winston

Starting a Small Business

Small business owners are what keep America running. There are over six million businesses with close to 97% having fewer than 100 employees, with most grossing less than a million dollars. So, when weighing up your future options, ask the question of whether self-employment is right for you. Why? Because, over time, you want to increase your income but work less, and working for yourself will do this. Your ultimate goal is to earn money while you sleep. You can also do what you prefer in life, so that you can indulge yourself and your family in everything you desire without the fear of running out of money, while still achieving your dreams by working in a career you're passionate about and good at doing.

Small business is working for yourself but it also entails saving by making investments that work for you as well. Every investment is a risk, but without risk there is no reward.

People who seek safety really are not living a fulfilling life. Their thought of safety is really an imprisonment. Remember that thinking that a job is security is really taking away your freedom. Most people really already know what business to own. All we have to do is be observant in our area. Have you ever gone through your town and said, "I wish they had a ____ around here." If you have others telling you the same thing, then that could be a sign for a potential business.

After some research, you can use other peoples' experience if you do not know how to operate the business and use other people's money to help finance it. But most people do not follow through because of self-doubt and skepticism from others. It is that hesitation that turns into procrastination. Then other things crop up in our lives, and we soon forget our plans. Then, no surprise, that business finally shows up in your town and you've missed your chance.

As stated earlier, I have my B.S. in business and my MBA in business. What a waste of money. If I knew what I know today, I might have skipped these degrees. I do have to admit that it does feel good to have these educational requirements, but for the most part, it is worthless in creating wealth. All college does is teach you how to learn, and it is valuable as it shows employers that you have the ability to learn quickly. I just did not know any better, and I had many jobs from working at FAO Schwartz to DHL, to selling window treatments and mortgages. It was not until I sold mortgages on straight commission that I understood that hard work could create wealth and that the harder I worked the more money I made.

A lesson learned the hard way in business is to have emergency cash for your expenses in business for at least three months and when you get started;

this teaches you to become frugal. As I get older, I continue to realize that the freedom of having no debt is powerful because it relieves stress. When times become tough, and the rollercoaster of life happens, you will be better able to handle the situation with less anxiety. To be debt free and have money in your pocket is to be free to do want you want. The freedom to leave your job, start a business or travel where you wish. A scary statistic today is that more people declare bankruptcy than graduate college. I am in the middle of learning this lesson as I write this book. I have had a "mutiny" within my company regarding my employees, and I am also in the middle of a transition to another company but I am short on capital. The banks are not lending money, so I am forced to use personal investments to sustain my business. So, just because I am writing this book does not mean that I do everything right. But you can learn from my lessons, which I gained through experience, research, and the teaching of others.

I am obsessed with becoming the best person I can be and the seeker of the truth. Looking back, my positive attitude would allow me to continue to think and innovate, and have faith that every month will be plentiful. It is true that this belief and positive mental attitude have sustained a long run of incredible revenue for me, but to think that I was not vulnerable to things outside my control was foolish.

Many times I have used money or possessions to bring me happiness, and it does not seem that I am alone since the average US citizen's buying power, including adjusting for inflation, doubled from 1957 to 2002.

We buy because we are driven by fear, boredom, the promise of exclusivity, the need for approval, greed, and desiring the unknown. That happiness can be brought to us by something outside of ourselves in materialism. I am not suggesting that having nice things is wrong, but when it hinders your progress for wealth, it is a problem. So, an exercise that everyone should do before they become business owners (or even if you have no interest in becoming a business owner) is this: first, I think everyone should create a personal balance sheet.

Second, a discipline that everyone should try for one month and trust me this is hard to do: write down and keep track of everything you spend. I am talking EVERYTHING. Keep a pad with you, and this will show you where your money goes and will give you appreciation of the decisions you make and you will find that some of them are foolish. The key here is to try to carry your pad or notebook around with you and keep a note of all purchases.

The true key to wealth is time, not money, so we work for time not money. The key is to have your money work for you. The truly wealthy never start a job that requires them to constantly work to make money. This is what the lawyer or doctor does not really get, unless they use leverage to help them or invest in businesses or investments with the wealth they have earned. There is only so much time in a day and you will always be limited to one special commodity: time. This is especially true for people who work for an hourly wage or salary.

We're often taught that we need to work harder in a job to get a better wage, or even take on a second job to reach our financial goals. Yet, by becoming self-employed, they lose control, which is the only thing in life that people have some control over. The key in the long run is to have other people work for you to create wealth, and not the other way around.

Leverage through Individuals

Starting up a business is not easy which is why 90% of all businesses fail within the first five years. You have to work very hard at first. Then once the business is established, other people can create that wealth for you. Thus, even though you might be sacrificing a lot of time in the beginning, it is only temporary.

What are businesses that can create income to you without being present, on site? Laundromats, being a franchise owner, real estate, royalties from a book, storage units, network marketing, coin-operated machinery. The point is that these add value to people and create wealth without you being physically there on a day to day basis. Also if you are to make money off of any business you start, the key is to use the proceeds to create more wealth through other businesses or investments.

Delayed Gratification

When I was younger, I remember my parents making fun of a gentleman in our area who had many properties and businesses. I will never forget the comment my mother made when I was about ten. She stated to me, "With all those businesses, you think he could afford a better car." Wow, knowing what I know today that was the wrong way of thinking. I say this because this man was truly reinvesting his proceeds or earnings, and today he has the last laugh. While my parents do not have two dimes to rub together today, he retired at 55. The last time I saw him, about ten years ago, he was riding in a Bentley. Delayed gratification, discipline, and doing the right thing were his keys to true wealth.

You see, your business can be successful, but it is only when you duplicate that success in different areas that you achieve true success. Also, very rarely do I see people become truly rich unless they have multiple streams of income or other businesses. Many times the key to starting other businesses is to keep your ears open. This means you might not have the expertise in that area, but someone else will. I overheard an accountant in my referral group talking about opening up a DMV that she had experience in running and all the required licenses. She just needed some cash to get started. So, for about $35,000, we opened up a DMV and I became a 50-50 partner with her. Today that DMV provides after expenses about a $100,000 a year.

Trading Time for Money is Very Tough to get Wealthy

That is why a lawyer is not as rich as some small business owners who lack an education. The only way for a single attorney to make money is when he is using his own time working or talking to a client. It's better to sell your knowledge through CDs or books or develop a product that takes lots of upfront time and effort but then relatively no time afterwards, with income continuing to come in.

You also have to understand the value of your worth and what really brings in money. Doing tasks that are not actually producing wealth or cannot be delegated is not productive and will make the journey longer for success and riches. This is just a fact, and too many people do busy work that can be delegated even if it is related to their job because it delays them from doing what they really know they should be doing. Examples are real estate investors who should be looking for properties and monies to invest in those properties. A management company could and should manage the properties. A bookkeeper could pay your bills and balance a checkbook.

Other Peoples' Money. OPM

There is no other way to get richer quicker than to use other peoples' money. A bank for example is other peoples' money. Leverage is the key to wealth and it can be achieved by using other peoples' money. Believe me, if you can be successful and prove to be successful, other peoples' money becomes easier and greater in amounts over time. The key is to find them and then build up a team that can provide a source of funds. How? This will be explained shortly.

One of the things you have to understand is that if you want to have riches you have to be in places where rich people hang out. Rich people are looking for opportunities just as you are. They also typically have the experience and connections to get the job done. Remember that an investor's experience can be just as useful as money.

I know of a gentleman who made major mistakes in a past investment in a restaurant, and his experience saved myself and my partners tens of thousands of dollars. You will be surprised by the number of times people I really did not know, just by asking for their experience and to just have lunch with me for a half an hour, were willing to give me advice. I have done this over a dozen times and one of the biggest obstacles is YOU.

We, as humans, are so afraid of rejection that we relive the rejections in our minds many more times than we will actually get rejected by just asking for advice. This especially works when you say that you admire what they accomplished and stroke their ego a little.

OPM not only refers to how to raise money, but it is a key to you making tons yourself by helping people create wealth. I like this because it truly is a win-win situation for everyone and it was one of the ways that created my wealth. I am sure that God approves of this as well, blessing other people and being rewarded for it.

Much of the OPM career has to do with selling. As a true matter of fact, selling is the key to wealth. It does not make a difference what product you have if you cannot communicate effectively to people and really get down to the emotions of why people should want or have things, because everything that we purchase is based on a need or emotion. Think about it. As a financial advisor, I need to express to clients why this product made sense and touch a basic emotion. Then once I got the client, I need to service them so they would not leave, create a win-win situation so they make money and collect a fee from them.

By adding on year after year, it increases wealth. Especially if the client was doing well, my fee was based off the new asset level. We should be rewarded for a job well done. Become a money manager and your profits are even greater, but again, you have to be able to sell and perhaps transfer or convince people to trust your wisdom on general investments. Early in my career, I was a great hunter, but ignored my existing clients because I was worrying about the next great hunt. What a mistake. I have found out that by servicing my client exceptionally well and setting realistic expectations on returns that this was truly the best way of receiving new clients through referrals.

Bank Loans

It is an odd thing. When you need the money you cannot obtain it, and when you really do not need the money, banks are willing to lend. As I write this, banks are ridiculous. They went from loaning out capital to anyone to being overly cautious. This is the tough part when it comes to starting a new business.

A golden rule is that when they are willing to borrow, set something up that has a definite time frame on your terms when you have the strength to negotiate. That means try to secure credit lines for lengths of time when things are going well. In the beginning, the key for most is to have an asset that you can use to collateralize. Also, the large national banks may be more difficult to deal with than local banks.

On another subject, when it comes to venture capital for your "great idea," remember that it is very difficult to get and do not assume that your idea is worth a million dollars. It could very well be, but most people think their idea is worth more than it really is. Any help or cash from experienced people with a proven track record, if they are willing to help you succeed, is priceless. The key when asking people who might give you money is to do the following:

1. These people are busy and, if successful, have heard all the bull crap before so get to the point.

2. Do not be afraid to persuade them and talk with confidence. If you are not confident, then it creates doubt in their mind that it is worth the risk.

3. Be honest, polite and give real figures when it comes to your sales and projections.

4. Do not be greedy! Large success cannot be maintained without the help of a team.

5. Do your research.

6. Share your goals.

A Word of Caution

One of the things that I want to warn all who are thinking about becoming self-employed is that before you decide what you want to do, do your own due diligence; because we humans want instant gratification. A great exercise that you can do is write down everything you can think of that might occur in the act of running a business and everything you can think of to handle a situation that might arise. Then relax. Why relax? Please remember that your unconscious mind always works to give you the answers that you seek.

We also want things to come easily with little or no work. Very rarely does this happen, and most people do not see the sweat behind what has happened. I hate to tell you this, but the 'get rich' schemes never work. If I could get a nickel for every get rich stock pick or business I have heard from my clients, I would have to say it would be in the five figures. Guess what, not one success story. It is even in the Bible from Solomon who states, "He that tills his land shall be satisfied with bread, but he that follows vain persons is void of understanding" (Proverbs 28:19).

The reason why most people do not do their due diligence is because it requires work. Another reason is arrogance, thinking you know better than everyone else and can do everything on your own. Also, when you do your own due diligence you help create a vision of where you are exactly going because it creates a road map rather than just having an idea of what you want to accomplish.

If you break things down into steps, it makes things seem more accomplishable. And if you have success with some of the steps, it creates the hope that you need to succeed. Moreover, patience is the key because there is always an incubation period before something comes to fruition.

The great thing about starting a business is that you do not have to become some genius and invent something. You do not even need to know how to run that business. You simply have to be conscious of what is in need in your area and then find the business to fulfill that need. The point is that if you do not know how to run it, you can always put together a team of people to do it.

Always make sure that you find people who complement each other's strengths. An analytical person is usually not a creative person, while the creative people who can see the big picture might miss the finer details.

Once everyone is in place then it is a simple matter of delegating whatever it is that needs to be done to that right person with the requisite strengths. The first step in this process is to get together and create a brainstorming session to come up with ideas. Also, always avoid the negative person no matter how bright that person is. Discouragement kills dreams more than anything else. That is why so much time was spent on the mentality section. Think positive, and stay positive.

Build and Maintain Contacts

Your team is important, but so are your business contacts. Treat them well. For example, have client appreciation events, or vendors events regularly like monthly wine and cheese get-togethers, special appreciation days and ask them to *bring a friend*. The people you will meet will be well worth the cost of the events.

As a financial advisor, this type of socializing, meet-and-greet events have been the best way for bringing in new clients. It is the same situation in my real estate dealings where people have learned of new properties, and my business dealings where people have converged to work on great ideas. Make yourself well known!

So, as an exercise think of three ways you can build new contacts for your business. Write them down and do it. It could be attending country club events, going to Chamber of Commerce meetings, inviting over co-workers, etc. There are many businesses that are franchises, already with proven strategies to succeed. I will give you an example. In my area restaurant franchises started coming in, but none of these franchises offered breakfast. So, I inquired to a franchise that offered this concept besides lunch and dinner. I then found an individual who ran franchise restaurants in my area and also found a partner who had the extra money to put into this opportunity. We all won; the gentleman who ran the restaurant became part owner, the other partner and myself all made money. We used other peoples' money by using the bank and the government through an SBA loan where we only had to put up 15%. What is even more incredible is that we opened up two other restaurants with only 10% down, required from the SBA due to changes under President Obama. (Most of the time you would need at least 25% down for a restaurant.) I leveraged not only my money, but, even more importantly, my time. It made sense to have the gentleman who ran restaurants as one of my partners even though he put up no money, because, as of today, he runs three successful restaurants and I do nothing but collect money.

Creating a win-win situation for everyone is a law to success. People will work harder when they profit from a company's success. That is why the free enterprise system such as in the United States and the recent success of China, proves the point over countries such as Cuba or the old Soviet Union.

START-UP: WHAT'S THE BIG IDEA?

You can start a business that is a new idea, rather than an existing model. However, you have to have a vision if you want to do this and have very tough skin because most people will tell you it cannot be done. You need a great supporting staff with strengths you do not have, and be able to delegate to those people who have those skills.

Even if you can have the greatest idea in the world, if you cannot sell it, as they would say on the Sopranos, "forget about it."

And if you lack these skills to sell the idea to others, then hire a commission-only sales person and pay them *very* well.

Let's go back to vision; make sure it is a vision that will be relative in the future and you will be fulfilling a need. Raising capital could be difficult in this area, especially with the sharks who are the venture capitalists.

A very good and probable technique is to give a small part of your company to a shark to raise capital. Of course, please save your biggest prospect for when you definitely think you have worked out all the kinks.

Talking about capital, sometimes people spend money on things they do not need like a huge office to impress people. Think about raising money and showing success before spending it on overheads you do not really need.

Banks and the Government

First, before we even begin about talking about the details of how to use this form of OPM, be sure to *shop around*. Visit at least three different banks when deciding to borrow from these sources and develop a relationship with them, but always shop.

First step before you approach any institution is to develop a business plan. You do not have to know how to write a plan; there are many people who can help you or do this for a living, so just ask your accountant. As stated, life is a game of interest rates.

The key with OPM is to borrow at lower rates and invest the proceeds in higher rates. As I write this, the Small Business Association is lending money at 90% loan to value to expand your business, not the normal 20% typically required. On the $3 million that I was putting up, it saved me $300,000. That enabled me to put up another business for $1.5 million. So, see if there are government programs that you can utilize. Where do you find this information? Go to www.SBA.gov.

Common Mistakes

Not creating different entities for your business. For example, your building should be a different entity than your actual business. In our restaurant, for example, we have four entities. Real estate is a valuable asset that should be separated from the business which has more potential for liability. By doing this you can also gift ownership of one of the entities to your children but still maintain control of the business or real estate. This can also help out with retirement because you can still collect rental payments because you still have control even though you gifted the asset over to your children. Just remember, the more entities you establish, the harder it is for the creditors to attack your assets and wealth.

THE NO MONEY EXCUSE

Let me tell you how I raised my net worth to a few million with no money out of my pocket, but by just keeping my ears open. I knew of an individual who owned prime land, worth about $1.5 million, in my area which happened to be free and clear. He asked me one day about any opportunities that were available for a franchise restaurant. I said that I would look around. Well, there was an individual whom I knew who ran many franchise restaurants but had no money. I proposed that the gentleman who runs the franchise and I split the profits, as he had the experience that franchises want. They want investors who are owner-operators and actually work the business. It does not make a difference if you have $20 million dollars, they want you to be actively involved because you might not care if the business goes bankrupt because it does not affect your net worth that much. This is especially true if you listen to my advice, and it is a separate company. The franchise cares. It is their reputation, and the key for them to create more wealth and success comes from having successful franchises. Plus he knows nothing about restaurants, and the last thing he wants to do is work 60 hours a week again. The land, building and profits are split 25%-25% while the individual who owns the land takes 50%. Everyone wins, the owner increases his net worth by putting up the building costs of about $1.8 million, and does nothing but collect profits from the business. The gentleman who runs the restaurant technically became a millionaire overnight with his share of the building and the land; he works hard but this time shares in the profits instead of giving the profits to the owner. Thus he puts in extra effort as he's a winner. I win by doing nothing but introducing them in the first place and own a stake in the land and building and getting 25% of the profits by putting up some small amount of money. I HAVE DONE THIS THREE TIMES, increasing my net worth by about $6 million, just by listening and putting together win-win situations for everyone involved.

Now some people who are reading this will say, "he is very lucky and it is one in a million that an opportunity comes along such as this." BULL, that is why the mentality part is so important, and I told you not to skip it because if you just become aware that you can put something like this together, it is amazing how your radar detector goes up and just spots these types of opportunities. It is like when you are about to buy a particular car - do you ever notice that you begin to see that same car all over the place? That is because your attention is focused on it.

You see, it does not make a difference if you do not have the resources, it is just about asking questions and putting together people so that they can benefit each other, and of course, provide a service for the community. For example, when we built the chain, we picked one that serves breakfast, lunch and dinner. We did this because the other franchises that were being built were only serving dinner and maybe lunch, so there was a need (breakfast) that needed to be filled in the community.

Now coming up with a new concept can be more profitable than buying a franchise, but why do I encourage people to buy a franchise? Because they typically have proven strategies, proven procedures, and training available. These three things are critical for success. So, you do not have to think up an incredible idea because incredible ideas are everywhere; just make sure your idea fills a need.

It is very simple, did you ever get frustrated and say, "Darn, I cannot believe they do not have a __ in this town." There is an opportunity right there, the opposite of this is saying to your friend, "Don't worry about that, there are one of those almost every block, you should have no problems getting what you want." Once you find that need, do not be afraid of approaching people, because rich people are always looking for help, even though most people do not believe this to be true. I did this with a second restaurant and with a child activity center that was badly needed in my area, all with big success.

Effective Partnering

This is the key to getting what you want or accelerating the process. Almost any truly great success can be tracked down to effective partnering with someone who pushed the entrepreneur along. That is why I believe everyone that truly wants to succeed should put down those fiction books and read autobiographies of successful people. You will notice that Walt Disney and Rockefeller, for example, would not be who they turned out to be without partnering. Steven Spielberg was not a brilliant straight A student with gifts that everyone noticed immediately. The fact is, Spielberg was a C student and was rejected from film schools in California such as UCLA.

You also need to understand what your strengths and weaknesses are. Only then can you complement what you are lacking to make you and your partners an unstoppable team. If you have a lack of time or a lack of money, partnering is certainly the way to go. Even if you have lots of both, partnering is the right thing to do because you can be more effective and we all have weaknesses that can be eradicated by partnering with an individual who has that quality as a strength.

A quote from Jerry Weintraub in his book, *When I Stop Talking You Will Know I'm Dead*; he said that "relationships are the only thing that really matters in business and in life." Also one of the keys in his life was, "somehow I attracted mentors."

A good thought to remember is that the more you are concerned about your own happiness, the less fulfilled you will be – there is nothing better than helping others achieve their dreams as well as you fulfilling yours.

Partnering not only means partnering for business but having partners for all areas in your life such as relationships. I remember a friend seeing a marriage counselor who was himself married three times. Perhaps there can be better partners to show you success than a veteran of at least two divorces? The point is to seek a partner if possible who has already achieved some success in the area in which you are looking to succeed. A role model that you can aspire to.

One of the keys to locating effective partners is to find people who have the strengths that you do not and that means understanding what type of person you are. If you are a perfectionist, you tend to believe that success brings you happiness and you can be vulnerable to mood swings, because any rejection or setback that could separate you from your goal is a threat to your existence and failure is unacceptable to you. You also like to control the situation and are not able to relax until what you wanted to accomplish that day is done. Therefore, having another perfectionist on your team who does the exact thing that you are trying to accomplish could be counterproductive and not efficient.

You can find several mentors right at your fingertips. I'm talking about on book shelves, where famous and successful people openly discuss their failures and try to explain to you what to do differently.

THE MOST IMPORTANT THING IN EFFECTIVE PARTNERING is to partner with people who do not possess your strengths. We are all attracted to people who we have a lot in common with. This is evident in high school. However, you need to know your own strengths and know the strength characteristics of the others you work with. It is imperative to realize your strengths and definitely your weakness. By knowing your weaknesses you will have the ability to actually help yourself and self-improve just by being aware of what you are not. For example, I am impatient, I have a hard time relaxing, I am not the best listener and I give solutions right away instead of hearing others complete their thoughts. I am impulsive, too blunt, very demanding, and I can bully those slower to act or take responsibility. I have a problem relaxing because I always feel that if I am not active I will not reach my goals. How does this help me? Well, when I am about to act, I look back at my weaknesses and evaluate how I will act in this next situation.

There was a time when I went through many employees because I was impatient. I would not give them time to train, my words were too blunt, occasionally saying comments that were inappropriate about their job performance, and I was not listening as to why they were struggling at their job. When I started realizing these flaws in myself, I became more patient and a better listener and then, through listening, I found that some of these issues were simple to correct and my turnover stopped.

Knowing yourself, your strengths and weaknesses, will help you to be effective in finding the right partner. This technique also can be used for communicating with your spouse and children as well.

Here are some of the most common personalities and their strengths and weaknesses:

A. The Servant: Strength - Wants to be liked. Enjoys giving pleasure to others and seeks that acknowledgment. Likes to take care of others and care for them. Weakness – Can use their giving to manipulate others and have low self-esteem and insecurities. Also, will not correct an outcome or step in to correct a situation for fear of being disliked. It takes a great offense in order for them to act.

B. Achiever: Strength - wants to succeed, goal oriented and the opposite of a procrastinator. Sees most things as a "to do" list and cannot rest unless it is accomplished. Sees the end results and reacts quickly. Weakness – selfish and will use people and resources to better achieve their goals.

C. Analytical: Strength – Logical. Thorough, evaluates and does not make quick decisions. Attention to detail. Perfectionist. Weakness – slow to act, there is never the right time unless everything is perfect. Arrogant and hard to reason with. Not open to alternatives.

D. General: Strength – a great leader that inspires others. Wants and desires to achieve something great. Able to break down projects to tasks and follow up with accomplishments. Sees the big picture, hard worker. Weakness – has a desire for power and does not have compassion for those who are not able to perform to their standards. Impatient and sometimes quick tempered.

E. Old Faithful: Someone who is very loyal and loves being part of a team. Willing to sacrifice for the team and please the upper chain of command. Will go the extra mile and be counted on. Weakness – needs to keep focused on what is important. Not creative, not willing to make decisions.

When people think of partnering, they think of have a 50/50 partner or 4 partners at 25%. However, remember a partner can come in all shapes and forms; it could be an employee, advisors such as a good accountant, CFP®, banker, realtor, an author who specializes in an area you need, etc. Tell co-workers, friends and your partners who you are looking for and ask them what type of partner they are looking for. If they do not know, there is a great thing called the Internet. The key is that when you find that person who can change your life, make them the best offer you can and make sure that your presentation is effective. People want to protect what they have and want to always grow for gain in some way.

Morals should be without question, very important, but many people get caught off track persuading themselves that they are not that bad. I did this with a money manager who paid me more than others and made things very convenient for me from an administrative standpoint. Unfortunately, this cost me a lot more money because of his performance and his lack of care towards my clients made me lose some long-term relationships.

The key to finding out the type of person you are is the joy that you receive from doing certain activities, it comes with ease, you feel energized, time does not matter, you have a strong focus, you are happy, strong. Always try to work from strength to strength. If the activity drains your energy then you simply know it is not a characteristic or strength you have. This would be a void that a partner can fill.

By the way, even though you think that you want things to just be easy, you really are seeking challenges, because challenges excite us, energize us and make us feel great about our being, and gives you a sense of value. The skill level of any task has to challenge you. The key is to think of any task in these terms and not to allow it to overwhelm you.

Frustration and anxiety come to a point when the task might be too great for your abilities. The fact is nothing is too great for your abilities. It is all a state of mind. However, when you are struggling, this could be a calling to bring in a partner.

In the words of Romans 5:2-5 NIV, "We rejoice in the hope of the glory of God. Not only so, but we also rejoice in our sufferings, because we know that suffering produces perseverance; perseverance, character; and character, hope. And hope does not disappoint us, because God has poured out his love into our hearts by the Holy Spirit, whom he has given us."

The key is not to allow disappointment to creep in and take hold; it will paralyze you into no action when many times a partner could've resolved it. That is why in any business, hope and faith are important. Perseverance and hope bring us closer to God. Furthermore, remember that the struggle we are going through is only temporary. The problem-free life is boring because it does not allow us to grow, it lacks excitement. So, embrace the challenges and trust that you will overcome them.

The key in life is to continually grow. If you are negative at 20 years old, then if you do nothing about your attitude, you will still be negative at 50 and 90. Too many people search for that "perfect" task that will fit just right, but fail to act and are always searching. The key is not only to express our love for our family but in the tasks that we do every day, including work. I remember a book called *The Purpose Driven Life* and, to me, work is the primary place of where your calling gets lived out.

We all think of "thinking big," but unless we partner with someone, the goal of reaching something big is limited. If there were truly keys to success, finding smart people with ambition has to be one of them. Also, to realize when to leave a partnership when it has runs its course or if they outgrow what you can offer them as far as challenges and perhaps even money. Counsel is key and rejecting counsel, we will get what we think is right, but a lot of times it will lead us down the wrong path. If you reject criticism because of pride, you are being foolish. It might not always be right, but the key is to always take it under consideration. When giving criticism, be careful of your choice of words because it can break the spirit. Say some words of encouragement then choose careful words that are not harsh, but convey the message. Then end with some type of praise.

Everyone needs counsel. Without counsel, your chance of succeeding falls dramatically. What is important is finding the right counsel! The right counsel will be individuals who have integrity, a person who can be reasoned with, and a person with a track record of success in the area you are looking for.

But be careful because there are many with no track record but major potential. The key (and it is a big key) is that when you find the person do research about him or her and have a presentation put together that will show them how partnering with you will provide THEM with a benefit! In most situations sharing the financial wealth is what is necessary. Desire for gain is a big motivation for people, too, as is the fear of loss. Insurance companies make billions off this concept. Be careful with the fear concept, it will work in the short-term with employees but in the long run it makes people less committed, and less motivated. Always follow up with a thank you.

Counsel is not only related to business but your personal life as well. When I was separated from my wife relying on my old habits would have surely concluded in divorce, but I sought counsel from professional and a few Christian friends on how I might want to respond or handle situations.

As well as using mentors in my life, I have returned the favor and mentored others. When people ask me, I really feel genuinely honored and will offer my advice with little hesitation. An almost always sure way to gain their cooperation is to find out what the mentor wants and reciprocate by helping them get what they want.

One of the main qualities that others seek from me, whether as a mentor or as a partner, are my skills as a sales person. The key to selling anything is to fulfill the need and to make others understand that you can help them fulfill that need. Always remember that people will pay you if you make their lives easier. So a good technique when trying to make people understand that you can help them is to repeat back what they stated they needed. Always appeal to their emotions, if you can connect to their emotions, you will succeed 90% of the time. The key to prepping them about what you are trying to state is to appeal to their curiosity. For example, "what if I can show you an investment product that will give you the growth you are looking for, but if the markets do not perform well can also give you a guarantee?" Then relate the product to something such as a feeling/experience they had in the past, or someone they know that had that experience. For example, Mr. Smith might have seen his boss who retired five years ago go back to work because of bad advice/investments. You will only grab their attention or change their thinking or behavior by appealing to their real feelings or a situation that they can relate to.

Remember that people are motivated by gain, loss or to be loved. Also, if you have members on your team who become easily offended or always try to defend their positions sometimes by expressing it in anger – then it is time to sever your relationship with them.

In closing this chapter, a key to remember is to have different lines or fishing lines/business in your water because life becomes a lot easier with multiple streams of income. For many, instant gratification will be the cause of failure; for others, it will be self-doubt and procrastination.

The lines in the water can vary from real estate, stocks and mutual funds, to network marketing. As of now, energy seems to be a decent bet that is making many people successful. The key is to look for opportunities by asking empowering questions such as, "what is in need in my area that could help produce income?" not "why is life so hard, and I have to struggle?" not "why does bad luck follow me?" but "what good or what lesson can come from this?" Keep asking the questions and the answers will come.

By asking these questions you brighten your day or help control your emotions to make you more at peace and a positive person, which will enable you to become the best person you can become. Instead of allowing others to control your thinking, you take back the control.

I wish there was a way to be able to record the conversations in our minds, or questions we ask internally to ourselves because many will see why some are more successful than others. If we could suppress the negative feelings and replace them with positive feelings by using self-control, we would all become a lot more powerful. Doubt and procrastination are enemies of human advancement.

Work for Yourself: REAL ESTATE

First rule of getting into real estate is a team: a bank that you've become familiar with, an accountant, a contractor, good property manager, an attorney, a CPA and some realtors. Anyone with hard work and a dream can succeed in real estate. Another rule is there never is a bad time to invest in real estate. If the housing market is tough like it is as I am writing this book, then interest rates are probably low because of a weak economy and house prices are down. Just like in the stock market, you want to buy low and sell high. When houses are not selling, you can pick up great bargains. It really is common sense and when interest rates are low, it is a good time to rent. When prices are high and the real estate market looks good, then selling properties and flipping makes sense.

This is why we focused on your mentality, earlier in this book, because often people become paralyzed when buying real estate for the first time outside of purchasing their main home. It can be a different story when buying a piece of real estate for investment purposes.

I love real estate, however. Where else can you buy something for $100,000 and it only cost you $20,000 or less. By the way, they also give you tax breaks for owning them. Plus appreciation of about 5 percent a year. Small to medium priced houses are the way to begin for investors. Trust me, they will always be in demand. Affordable housing is within everyone's reach. Example: buy a house for $70,000. The mortgage payments are $375 plus taxes and insurance of $250 a month. You rent it out for $900 a month, get a tax deduction and appreciation of about $3,500, all this for money down of $14,000. That is a return of 23% not including appreciation and tax benefits. Not bad at all. It takes time and patience. That is the key to becoming wealthy in real estate. The more you know about real estate and the more experience you gain, the more successful you will be and the less risky it becomes. Yes, you still can buy real estate with 10% down.

Some rules of thumb:

1. Get about 1% in rent. A $100,000 home would mean a $1,000 a month in rent. That rent increases over time while mortgage payments stay the same.

2. In really depressed markets like we saw in 2009 and 2010, lots of bank deals were 20-30% less than the true market price of the home. Get financing from the same bank at low rates and then rent them to Section 8 government housing paid for by the government. 10% under market value is a good rule of thumb. Always take into consideration the cost of taxes and insurance, also dues.

3. In a good market there are still distressed sellers. There will always be divorces and financial distress in any type of market.

4. Real estate beats inflation. Much better than leaving money in a money market.

5. Check to see if the property is in move-in condition. If not, find out what the repairs will cost. (Use the contractor to give you the cost – he should give the estimate for free since you will be paying him for the job.)

6. Can you rent the property? Is the demand for rental property high? Ask a realtor or place an ad and see the responses you get.

7. You can find the deal but cannot afford it. Then do not worry, there are people who will pay you for finding properties for them. I am one of them. It is called Other People's Money or if you have equity in your house. You can use this equity to buy properties. The amazing thing is that through time you can create equity in your properties to use to purchase more properties. Tip - Never pull out 80% of the money your house is worth.

8. If you can find it and afford it but do not want to manage it then use your contractor or real estate agent to collect the rent for a share of the rent price or the opportunity to sell the property with them. (10% is a good management fee.) Also a management fee could be tax deductible if it is an operating expense.

9. Tax certificates are sometimes overlooked. Someone does not pay their taxes, you can buy it and they have to pay you interest. REITS are published on the stock exchange and you could also be a mortgage/bank for people looking to buy real estate.

10. If interest rates are two points lower than your current rate, refinance is typically the answer, even if small costs of about $500 are involved.

11. Shop around to at least 10 banks. Also, keep track of them at least every four months. Banks offer deals and change rates and fees just like any other institution. Save a few hundred here and there and it adds up over time.

12. Last resort, but I did this years ago to pick up a property from a couple who really needed the money from a divorce and flipped the property four months later for a quick $40,000 profit. That answer for me, at the time, was borrowing money from my 401(k).

13. Credit cards could be the answer. This is very risky but could be helpful. A friend of mine borrowed $5K that he needed for 0% financing for six months. Now he had a bonus that paid off that card at the year end from his employee, but it did enable him to close on a deal that he would have lost if he did not have the cash.

14. Private lenders: remember, though the rate will be higher, about 3% higher than a typical loan, it is worth it if the rent still covers the payments to the lender.

15. Each property should be a separate LLC. You own five properties. Someone slips and falls on one and they can sue you and include the other four properties. Slip on your LLC and they can only sue you for that entity and not the other four properties that are separate LLCs.

16. Attend real estate meetings or clubs. The people there have either money or the ambition to learn. Call the National Association of Real Estate clubs or use the Internet. Most people have money but not the time so trust me it is a lot easier to find people who can give you the money.

17. Use an attorney to draw up your partnership agreement. Do not try to save a dime to be dollar foolish and forget something important that puts you in a bad situation.

18. Place an ad in the paper describing what you are looking for. Laugh at this but a good friend of mine closed on over 26 deals in 14 years using this strategy.

19. Real estate auction. You will certainly come across people who need a partner. Sometimes you can find a partner right there who will help you. This is easy pickens. However, the key here is to bid with your brain not your heart, getting caught up in the emotions of the auction. Look for auctions on foreclosed or bank owned properties. For sure, you will be going against people who know what they are doing and have experience bidding at these auctions. Just look in the paper for when these auctions occur; they might be held at the property, court house, or local auditorium. You really can get great bargains because this is a last resort for most institutions to get rid of decent properties they do not want. Make sure it is an "absolute mortgage" meaning that the home must be sold regardless of price. If not then, for most, it is not worth attending. Do your homework, find out the properties listed and what price you will pay for each. Look at comps in the area. Have money available to put down. A good amount would be about $10,000. If you win, contact your attorney to help you with the paperwork. Always include a written statement in your writing that "the document is subject to your attorney's review." If they do not accept – do not sign. If you lose to someone, sometimes these bidders do not come through, so you can get on a list in case that happens called "the right of first refusal" – ask to be on that list. You can use an auction to sell your home for a fee of about 2% but probably will not get the best price that you are looking for. Essentially, these people are there for bargain properties.

20. The government. Yes the government. I have no experience in this area but let me tell you what I know. First contact the United States General Services Administration. Ask to be sent a copy of the U.S. Real Property Sales list or go online to be sent a list. They do not send you a continuous list. You have to request it through a card they provide with the list. Remember that professionals will be at this event so be prepared to do your homework. Cheap homes are HUD homes that are great rental opportunities. These are houses that were

defaulted on and the government has possession of the homes. Call your local HUD home and find the local banks that they work with; some of these homes could be bought with as little as 5% down. You might have to make a bid and many times the financing can come from an FHA loan. What is great is that many times, HUD will pay some of the closing price and the brokers' commissions. The rates are very attractive and if you buy the property for cash you could get very good deals.

21. Government-seized properties that were bought, stolen, etc. from illegal activity. This is something that I would like to have a go at in the new year. Contact your local Customs office. The United States Marshall Service seizes assets that can be sold. Check your paper, they are required to advertise the auctions. You can get data sheets of the property description. Sometimes the properties are odd sizes but might be able to be used, for example, if someone needs to put up a billboard if the land is close to the highway.

22. If you have no money and were a vet, then through the help of the government you can buy a house with NO money. If you are a first time home-buyer, for a limited time in 2013 you could buy a house with no money down as well. Just find out how much money you are paying in rent or would pay for rent and buy a home that is the same payment with taxes and insurance included. I am amazed at how many people do not take advantage of such opportunities. Some use the excuse of not being in the area for a long period of time, let's say one year. Who cares if you have no money down? Also, call your local government office and look for Grants. Or for low income earners through Section 235 buyers can buy a home and have some of their mortgage paid by the government. Also there are vets who default on their homes, so call the local VA Department and get a listing of such deals. The VA will pay the real estate brokers' commissions, so try to work closely with a realtor who specializes or has experience in this area. The down payments on VA homes are low, close to $1,000 and are typically in low cost neighborhoods so this is typically a great rental market. These houses are usually listed 15-20% lower than market prices, and sold typically on bid prices. So, the realtor will be able to tell you what other prices are listed at that are comparable so if you know the house is discounted then bid about 5-7% above what the house is going for to win the bid. The only problem with VA

properties is that they need a little tender loving care which means like any home you purchase, have a home inspector give you an estimate of the costs.

23. There are organizations and grants available for people who want to buy homes in urban areas to help rejuvenate those areas.

24. Become the bank, the mortgagee. This is a great way to make sure the property is kept in great condition. You come up with the down payment and the partner lives in the home, takes care of it and then you split the property profits when the home sells. This works very well when helping out family members get a start and everyone wins. You can advertise this in the newspaper as well or tell the real estate club or realtors what you are looking for. This is a sure way of making certain that your home is in good shape and ready to sell. This is a GREAT way of getting many offers! You get your down payment back and split the property home sales above the original price, or the profits. Include a clause that will let them buy you out. Meaning if they fell in love with the home, then you can bring in an appraiser, they pay back your down payment and split what the house has appraised to. They can usually get the money they need to pay you by refinancing the home especially if time passed and the home appreciated considerably. If your partner does not pay the mortgage, you have a right to take it over and rent it to someone else.

Have an attorney draw up the deal and put in the contract "deed in lieu of foreclosure" so if things go sour you can easily get back the home. Also, make sure the deal is for a certain period of time - somewhere between 5 and 10 years so you could actually reap some of the benefits. I like the idea of becoming a mortgage holder or second mortgage holder. You can get a good rate of return and have it secured, which is important to the owner. Be careful not to give a second mortgage if the equity is not there. 60% loan to value is max as far as I am concerned. For example, if the house is worth $100,000 and there is a first mortgage of $40,000 do not loan more than $20,000 in a second mortgage. You want to make sure you are getting your money back and this should be OK for a depressed market and a quick sale if it comes to that. The term of paying it back should be less than 10 years. There are many people who are carrying second mortgages for people who only got approved for a certain amount of money so the owner gave them a second mortgage to help them. You can buy the second mortgage from the owner at a discount. The owner might just want to not have the hassle because they moved, for example, or have promised a loan for 15 years and does not want to wait that long to get paid back.

Always use an attorney to check for liens you might not be aware of and other matters and such things as an estoppel certificate (don't worry, your attorney will know what it is). Also, try to stick to small properties instead of large commercial or residential properties. And furthermore, just like in buying a new home, make sure the property is desirable or something you would buy to rent out. How you find the second mortgage holders is by putting an ad in the paper. You will be surprised at how many people have used this to sell their home.

25. With interest rates at an all-time low, it is very hard to find a CD that will keep up with inflation. As of the beginning of 2013, you cannot really find one. If you want an investment that is better rate then a CD and just as safe, look towards a Tax Certificate. These are from people who have not paid their real estate taxes. You basically are paying the taxes for the individual who defaulted and get the interest due to you above what the taxes due are. Rates can be as high as 8-10%. Most of the time, the owner pays the taxes so he does not lose the home. There are postings at the court house and all you have to do is call. A great idea if you have a tax certificate is to contact the owner because he might be having some financial difficulties and might be interested in selling the home. If not, you typically have to hold the certificate for a few years, then it goes to foreclosure where you can then bid on the home. The good news is that you are the first in line to buy the property.

Real Estate usually is a good investment in an inflationary time because it typically moves directly with inflation.

The first rule to remember is that residential real estate is easier to buy and sell. Remember though, real estate is not a double-wide home. It depreciates sort of like a car while true real estate appreciates.

Also, location is the most important factor, a highly desirable area, such as owning rental property near a University. Another rule of thumb is to buy the worst house in the best neighborhood rather than the best house in the worst neighborhood. Live by these rules.

Moreover, try to find homes that look bad but really only need cosmetic surgery such as new rugs, painting, refacing the cabinets, etc. By the way, always have your house inspected, you will be amazed at what this can save you over the long run.

If possible, look for a sellers' concession. Typically the seller will give you back, let's say, 2% of the sales price at closing to help you settle closing costs such as attorney, taxes and insurance costs. You also need to know about assignment clauses. Meaning how we could tie up a property for a certain amount of days such as 60 or 90 days for a little amount of money, sometimes as little as a dollar, and resell the property at a higher price during this time with you keeping the profits. But the point here is that this is not limited to just real estate, this can be used with any property.

I have a friend who does this on Ebay and Craigslist and gets money deposited in his Paypal account all the time. Just make sure you include the assignment clause. Talk about a great way to get money to use for real estate. I have a friend who through EBAY sold $5,000 worth of stuff he does not even use including golf clubs, baseball cards and a doll collection his mother left him. He used the profits to come up with money for a down payment on a house by selling the stuff online in less than two weeks. (By the way he sold the property two months later and made a nice $30,000 profit.)

Sources to get the Money to Buy

1. Outside hard money lenders. I once bought a property by borrowing the money from a gentleman who wanted a return of 10% for the monies borrowed and got the rest from a bank. Because of the steep discount I bought the property for, the rent covered both payments. Typically you can find these people in your local newspaper. Also if they are willing to give you the money, if they are experienced in lending money, then it could give you the indication that you've found a good deal.

2. The banks. Here is what the banks are looking for, basically three things that you have to remember: LTV – Loan to value. Let me give you an example, your house is worth $300,000, the banks will only loan you up to 70% of what your house is worth (LTV). Thus if you have a first mortgage of $100,000, you then can borrow an additional $110,000. Now different banks have different lending guidelines and I am always surprised to see that most people only go to one bank and then give up. (Part one mentality again.) Though guidelines have been tighter than in the past, I have seen banks still go up to 90-100% of what the properties are worth. Even though the government, as I

write this, is being very aggressive with businesses and the SBA is letting you expand your business with as little as 10% down, 90% LTV. That is a fantastic deal, so while most people are unaware of this and think lending guidelines are tough right now, they do not even know that this opportunity exists. Please remember that when the economy is tough there are many opportunities to be had because the government especially is looking for you to start producing again so that the economy can recover.

The second thing they look at is credit or FICO score as some people refer to it. The bottom line is that your credit has to be pretty good, NOT PERFECT but pretty good. Banks will listen to explanations. This should never deter you though if you have partners. Their credit scores could carry yours.

The last thing is debt to income ratio. What they simply do at this stage is look at your income and the debt to that income. If it is too high, let's say over 60%, they will turn you down. So if you make $4,000 a month and your bills are $3,000, this could be an issue. Showing no income has become very difficult to do if you want a loan, but remember that the bank will take into consideration rental and investment income.

I know that things are tough in the banking industry as I write this book, but I am confident that when things get better, banks will loosen up their guidelines, competition will occur, and some of the old ways of lending will come back into play. The 80/20 mortgage is a good example. This is where you borrow 80% of the appraised value from the bank, and then take a second mortgage for the other 20%. If you cannot borrow the full 20%, then come up with 5% and see if they will loan you 95% LTV. Of course you need good credit, but the key is avoiding the mortgage insurance, called PMI, if you put down less than 20%.

There are still mortgage renovation loans that loan you the money to buy the property and also give you the money to renovate the property through a licensed contractor. They will only go up to 90% LTV of the home.

A good source for finding money can be the equity you have built up. As stated before, leverage is the key to real estate and keep leveraging. As your cash flow continues to increase, use this extra cash flow to buy more real estate. Always try to use leverage. Leverage of money but that also means leverage of time. I had people look for places for me to then split the profits with little or no effort on my part, just to put up a portion of the cash. You can use other peoples' experience, as well as other peoples' ideas to drive your own success. I was interested in buying a building when my gym trainer came up with the idea of putting up a recreational facility for kids, which was in demand in our area. I brought in partners and used other peoples' money, experience, and talent to all chip in to make a win-win situation.

3. Another source of income can be the real estate agents themselves. Make an offer to purchase the property then ask if they can carry all or a portion of their commission on a note, with of course an attractive interest rate. On a $200,000 property that could be up to $12,000.

4. Sounds simple enough, yet it's worth considering buying a house well below the appraisal value. Example: I bought a home for about $150,000. The house was appraised at $225,000. I got 80% first mortgage with a 20% second mortgage and had about $15,000 to use for renovations then sold it for $253,000 with no money out of my pocket. It was worth about $265,000 but I sold it cheap so that I never made one mortgage payment because of a 60 day grace period before my first payment was due. You have to be careful because the price of this home for the area I was in was on the high side; I would have had a hard time getting rent to cover the mortgage payment. That is why houses in the $100,000 to $150,000 range are preferable.

5. The seller as your source of income, especially if they are selling the home on their own and it is free and clear. There are many properties like this. Lots of times the owner will take the proceeds and invest it in passive investments such as bonds and stocks. If you can agree to a term with an attractive rate that will meet or beat what these passive investments can give them. such as 10%-12%, then you can get them to pay for your down payment on your mortgage. In real estate terms, it means selling you the property and taking back a mortgage on it. The seller wins by making more on the property than they wanted to sell it for and can still use the property as collateral. This is especially attractive to the person selling the home; if you are going to make improvements to the home, how can he lose? This is also a great technique when you have a stubborn seller who wants nothing less than the full asking price and the house has been on the market for a while and he/she is having a problem selling it. (If the promissory note is longer than five years then the banks will treat the loan as a second mortgage.)

6. Vacant land – not a short term investment. You buy land to hold onto it to sell it in the future. This is if you have extra money on the side to wait. However, it should absolutely be part of your portfolio. Vacant land that can be subdivided can really be a great way to have a 'no money down' situation. Make an offer to buy the land at the cost they are asking or sometimes even above what they are asking.

When you make such an offer, ask the seller, because of the deal you are offering, if they will wait several months until you subdivide the land. I truly believe that an easy way to make money is to buy land, let's say 30 acres and then divide that land into 5 or 10 acre parcels. Have a local surveyor divide up the land into the sections for you. Always ask your attorney to include a clause of "partial release from mortgage clause" so that you can sell a portion of the land to someone else. I once did this and divided the lot in four sections. I sold two off immediately, which was enough to pay the full asking price. I offered the lots to these two individuals at a discount because they paid me up front and of course I needed the money. This can be hard to find, but where I am from with some farm land around, it is possible.

The key to vacant land is to buy it and hold it for 5-10-20 years. The bad part is that you pay taxes on it, and it is harder to sell than a home, but the good part is that there are no calls to fix anything or collect any rent. Good land can double every 7 years in value. Urban land is the best, and you want to think of holding it for 10 years. Also do not be afraid to buy land in a different state than yours but not with real estate if you are a beginner. Remember you always have to see the land yourself.

Just like real estate, compare prices with raw land just like you would with a home. Go to the local courthouse and investigate records of similar land sales in the area. Make sure you can have a septic system on the property or it has access to public waters, and just like a home, always have it inspected by a person who is a Member of the Appraisal Institute or from the American Society of Appraisers. Check to see that it has a clear title, always use an attorney, make sure it has adequate draining of water, does it already have a survey on it, etc. The key to raw land is trying to predict where people are migrating to. Unlike in investments where inside information is illegal, the good thing about real estate development is that it is not, so find out as much as you can from anyone that knows what is about to occur in the area you are thinking about purchasing. Think about where people are moving to, check out the local Chamber of Commerce and ask questions about communities where people are moving to, what major corporation or project is being built nearby, and read your local paper for the latest news and developments in the area. That will tell you what is proposed on the table that might be built. Also, have a relationship with a broker who will apprise you of things that are happening in your community.

Use common sense as well, for example, streams through a property is always nice and adds value to your property. Look online at places such as American Society of Farm Managers, Farmers National Company, *Field and Stream*, the local newspaper, and many other places that will tell you about raw land for sale.

When you ask to buy the land, ask if it is registered and ask for the property report. Do not forget about tax certificates for raw land. This is my hidden secret. Just like with real estate, do not be afraid to ask the owner to finance the land for you and pay him an attractive rate. People are more flexible with land than they are with buildings. Do not pay the sellers' points or closing costs and, with rates very low at this time, the technique of asking the owner to finance the land for you is very attractive, especially with money market rates at 1% right now. Also, if you are going to a bank you might have to put more money down than on a home. For some reason, banks do not like raw land.

When selling your land, place signs high enough so that they cannot be stolen easily. Also think about owner financing it yourself. If you do finance it yourself, try to ask for the amount you paid for the land as the down payment since hopefully you bought it at a discount at wholesale prices. The rest is pure profit. Think about how great this is if you had no money out of your pocket because you found someone who will finance it 100% for you. Place ads in the paper and tell the public that you are selling the land by owner. People feel more comfortable that they are getting a good deal from the owner rather than a large organization where there is no room to negotiate.

7. Assumption of a mortgage. Some properties already have built in equity and the people are behind on their mortgage payments. If you can save their credit, negotiate with the bank and assume the mortgage payments, then everyone wins. The bank does not want the home, the people save their credit, and in one case I even offered them an extra $10,000, and you buy a home with built in equity. I rented the home, actually had to chip in an extra $50 a month to pay the mortgage, but two years later when the real estate markets turned around, I sold it for a 33% profit.

8. You can make arrangements with the seller to take over the payments. You want to make use of an escrow company to make the payments instead of trusting that the seller would do so. One thing that could happen is if the bank finds out about it they can call in the loan immediately, but most banks do not care as long as they receive the payments. This technique works well when someone is in a hurry to sell their property. You can also get title to the property. The seller has to trust as well that the buyer will make the payments, if they do not, the seller can thank the buyer for any profits he made. This is very hard to do nowadays, but I have a friend who has successfully done this three times over the last five years.

9. Tax certificate and foreclosures. Where do you find tax sales? The Tax Collectors Assessor's or the Treasurer's Office. The lists are for public view, and there is a person called the section clerk who, by law, has to tell you the date on which the tax sales will take place or advertising when they will take place and where, such as what paper it will be advertised in. Be persistent, you have the right to this information and, as you already probably know, government employees are not the most cooperative people. Many times they can put you on a list to receive the information. Writing a letter asking to be put on a list could be effective sometimes. Banks tend to guard these properties like they are producing a large revenue for their coffers. Yet, this is something that does not make sense to me, as you could be a possible solution to taking the property off their hands.

What you need to do is visit the bank personally. That is why I said it is important to get to know your bank well. When you visit the bank, ask for the foreclosure department or who is in charge of non-performing assets. Unfortunately, you might have a hard time getting a name. I get around this by getting friendly with the branch manager at the bank who could give me a name, or try to own a part of the bank. How do you do that? Buy some stock, you can say that you are a stock holder and have a right to look at the institution's accounting records regarding foreclosures. Also the paperwork is a pain, so call up agencies and ask for brokers who have experience with the paperwork. One way to get foreclosures before they happen is to advertise in the paper that you "buy houses before they go into foreclosure." Offer slightly more than what is owed on the mortgage; enough for the owner to walk away with some cash to get a fresh start. There are lists that are at the courthouse of pending foreclosures and remember that this is public information. There are even companies that will sell you foreclosure lists.

How do you approach the owner? By letter can work best, by saying that you want to help them get out of their situation and possibly put some cash in their pocket to get a fresh start and save their credit as well. It really is a win-win situation, as you get a great deal and you help a person in need. You can sometimes even have them pay you rent until they decide to move. You could even agree to help them out of the situation by becoming equal owners with them so that when the property is sold you get paid back plus a share in the profit.

When banks cannot carry the cost of the foreclosed properties, they give them to Federal agencies who advertise the properties online and through major publications such as the *Wall Street Journal* and *USA Today* in their real estate sections. Some government agencies do bids only in writing.

Remember to treat foreclosures like you would any other property in that you get it inspected and make bids below what you are actually asking for. These houses will need some tender loving care so take into consideration the time and money needed to get these properties ready. There is still major negotiation that takes place – stick to your price!

Also when you are going to sell the home do not be afraid to list it while you are doing the repairs; most people wait, but that's a big mistake. List it for a profit and then, of course, tell the prospective buyer that you will raise the price once the repairs are done. The good news is that many of the banks will give you the mortgage to buy the home depending on if you meet their requirements, Debt to Income ratio, etc.

10. In the investment sections, we looked at a REIT (Real Estate Investment Trust). Well, you can do almost the same thing by getting partners together to buy real estate. For your work of arranging all the partners together, you can probably get your share for free since you added sweat equity. I know of a few people who got together 5 people, 10 people, and as many as twenty to buy property together with each owning equal or sometimes larger or smaller ownership according to their contributing dollar amounts. A partnership agreement through an attorney is necessary to discuss how the group will make decisions, when to sell, improvements to be made, and many other factors. When I was in graduate school, a friend bought two properties like

this without putting up any money himself. They sold one of the properties, and he made $40,000 profit. He bought a home when he received his first job right after getting his MBA. Since he did not make a lot when he got his first job after college, it would have taken him at least 10 years before he had that size of a down payment. What's even smarter is that he took on roommates from work, which paid his mortgage. Pretty smart.

11. A good idea if you are not sure if you are going to live in the area or if you are first starting out, look into doing a lease to purchase. A client of mine fresh out of college did this. He rented for two years with the option to purchase the property for a certain price. Well, when the housing market took off, he noticed this trend and started looking for buyers while technically still renting. He found a buyer for $223,000. My friend had a right to buy it for $175,000. So, he borrowed the money from his dad, made a nice profit and paid back his dad an extra $5,000 for using his money for about three weeks. If you are a seller, you can consider this option. I have done this many times. You will see that typically people will treat the property better if they are thinking about buying it in the future. Also, you have a built in profit you can count on, especially if the market dips. Most of the time you will give back a small portion of the rent as a credit for buying the property. This is attractive when you do not have a lump sum, but can afford the monthly payments. This is also attractive if you can assign the lease agreement to another individual to essentially hold the property for you so that you can decide if you want to buy the property, depending on market decisions. Also, this is a desirable set-up if the property needs a little tender loving care. Many times you might not have enough for the down payment but have enough for the small repairs that have to be done. After you fix the house, you can then place it on the market for a substantial profit. The key here is to do your homework to make sure the property is undervalued or the eyesore in a nice neighborhood. Many times the owner will let you forgo the security deposit if you agree to fix up the property.

12. Being a landlord: This is something I am not great at, and I have people do this for me but here are some lessons I've learned: A. Always have your lease looked over by an attorney. They can explain the local eviction laws and limits on the rent you are charging. B. Get a list of Section 8 tenants from Housing and Urban Development. The gov-

ernment will help pay their rent for you. C. Advertise in the paper and always post a sign. D. Visit tenants close by and ask them if they know of anyone who might be interested and give them a referral fee for finding someone. Renters know other renters. E. Making up a flier and putting them in mailboxes works sometimes as well. F. Do not waste your time going out to show a property ten times. You want serious renters so charge a $25 screening fee. G. Check credit references of other places where they have rented. This is IMPORTANT. If people are good renters, they will surely have a reference. If they do not, do not allow them to rent from you. They will be a headache you do not want. H. You need their driver's license and check their social security number. I. Do not let them call you for every little chore like a blown out light bulb. List specifics on items for which the tenant is responsible. J. Let them know what hours they can call unless it is an emergency like a flood or no heat. K. Always make sure the first check clears before letting them move in. L. I try very hard not to raise rent on a tenant who pays well and I give discounts for paying their rent early. For paying on time, I also give a smaller discount. If late, I charge a penalty. Do the same. It motivates renters. Also set up a credit card machine. It takes away the excuse of not being able to pay the rent. M. Use an attorney to evict a tenant – do not do it yourself and always start the process early with no deviation. Especially if you own a property with multiple tenants, they speak to each other and you must treat everyone the same, as well as show them all that you mean business if they don't follow the rules.

Also as a side note, you need to be a little creative. I have a vacation home in Utah. I really wanted to take a vacation to Alaska and at the time could only afford the cruise and not the land excursions. However, I really wanted to do both. So, I rented my Utah home to seasonal skiers for two weeks and used the $4,000 to help with the land trip.

My fear of having the house destroyed was diminished when the agency that found the renters showed me pictures, and, of course, having a refundable $1,000 for damages helped. I actually learned this from a friend who uses his house in New York to do this. When he is planning to go on vacation, he rents his house out for the week to a person taking a vacation to New York.

13. Make sure you always have an assignment clause when buying a property. The longer time to have an option to close the better. I once

bought a great property for an awesome bargain and someone made an offer to me before I even closed the deal; I assigned the property and made a nice profit.

14. In down markets like what is occurring now, REO are very attractive, basically this is when the bank takes over a home from a buyer who cannot pay. Look to local realtors to find you good deals. You can place an ad in the paper as well during tough times, something that states you are "the answer to their prayers if people are behind on their mortgage." I made a deal with one client to get their mortgage up to date and make the payments on the property until it sold. Thus saving their credit and making a profit when the home sold. Again, do not be afraid to ask. You can buy these properties if you wait a few years and many times when the market turns around, you can make a nice profit. Also, remember that banks are not in the business of actually owning homes. So, if it is going to cost the bank more money in the long run, they will usually dump it for less money than it is worth. When talking to the bank, always include negative aspects about the property along with a contractor to give them estimates on the cost to repair the property.

15. When it comes to managing your property, the key is to keep good records especially when it comes to repairs. Also make sure you have a separate checking account for the properties. Always do a credit check on the tenant along with employment verification. If possible, always ask the last landlord about them. This will tell the whole story – trust me. Do not forget to take pictures before they occupy the property and have them check off from a checklist any things they see wrong with the property. Do not forget liability and umbrella insurance and, when you have more than ten tenant properties, think about hiring a property manager. Make sure the tenant puts in writing any problems and never allow them to discount it off their rent. Otherwise, they will abuse this privilege and make sure they get at least two, preferably three, estimates.

16. Partnerships. I have been in many deals where the person found the property, I put up the money, and we split the profits when they sold it. So, they used no money out of their own pockets. I have also been in a situation where I spotted a property but did not have any money. So, I kept my ears open at social events and contacted these individ-

uals who had the cash for the properties, and we split the proceeds when we sold it. People are too greedy and many want everything for themselves, but if you can find a true win-win situation, then most people will follow - especially if you make money for them. I was glad to put up the money for those deals. They found the property, fixed it and sold it. I put up my money for a few months and made a nice profit by doing nothing. There have been deals that have not sold quickly, so always have a second strategy such as renting the property. If you rent the property and it still does not make sense, then do not do the deal.

LOCATION, LOCATION, LOCATION. I will mention location again. Because it is very important! One rule of thumb is to make sure the property is not more than an hour away. Why? Maintenance and finding tenants. Also, the neighborhood should be desirable.

The key to partnering and finding a desirable property is to develop your team. A good realtor – both commercial and residential, a good CPA, a good mortgage broker, a good inspector, a good handyman, a good appraiser and, of course, investors. Once you find these partners, make copies of your tax returns and pay stubs. You would not believe how long it takes people to get these extra copies, especially if their CPA is on vacation or it is tax season. This delay of a week or two causes many to lose out on good properties.

Lastly, when mentioning partners, you should not forget friends and family as a source of cash flow. Be careful. Make sure that the deal is sound before approaching them. If you do prove that you can continue to bring them good deals, ask them for a favor and ask people they know who could support you. Also, never use the same attorney – that is, both of you and not every deal is 50-50. It is always negotiable. In the beginning, it might be that way just so that you can attract the partner. But if you are getting the deal, fixing the place, and selling the house on a very timely basis then you could negotiate a deal of say 70-30, and the same goes for the person who is only chipping in the money.

It all comes down to how much you could earn somewhere else. A great example of this is my friend Nathan who really had a good partner. In the beginning, he was splitting the money 50-50 with his partner, then the partner brought down the percentage to a 70-30 split where he was only receiving the 30%. Then his partner went down to 25% on a few deals. This upset my friend, and he foolishly dropped his partner. When I evaluated the deal it was very foolish.

The reason it was foolish was because, for a $50,000 down payment, they were making a $30,000 profit where he would receive $7,500 and of course his $50,000 back. Why this was a good deal was because he was making a 15% return $7,500/$50,000, and it only took them three months to buy the property, fix, and sell it. A 15% return in three months is incredible. If he could do this every three months it would be a 60% return on his money, even if it was $7,500 for the year; where else can you get that rate of return? In the stock market? Absolutely, but a 15% return in the stock market is a good return if you can average it a year.

Do not be afraid to have many partners in each deal. I have been involved in deals of 15 people or more. You have a general partner who is in charge of all decisions and really does all the work. All limited partners, everyone except the general partner, are limited in risk to the amount of money they contribute. You might be saying, "I do not know that many people." Well, what you can do is place an ad in the "Money Wanted" column that says simply, "Private investor seeking real estate deals with good returns and a safe position, call me with your deal at ####," or "Do you want to invest in a lucrative real estate deal but do not have the time or expertise? I have the experience, have lots of deals, but do not have the money. Please call me at ####."

In checking out your partner, do a few things: 1. A credit check. It will let you know what you are truly dealing with. 2. Ask for two references with telephone numbers whom you can contact. 3. If the deal is a large one, then a financial statement. So you know you are not wasting time on something that is unrealistic, because your partner cannot really pull it off, especially if you know what the banks are looking for. The key is to tell your partner upfront any situation.

I did a very lucrative deal with a partner once who went bankrupt because of an unscrupulous partner in a printing company. He told me upfront and had documentation proving his claims, and he turned out to be a very good partner.

17. Where to begin? Drive through neighborhoods. Look for "for sale" signs. Typically the "for sale" signs are the people most motivated to sell. They might need that 6% commission that a broker would receive. A word of advice - if you took a vacation and checked out the properties in South Carolina; they are a lot cheaper with lower taxes. But, of course, remember: location, location, location. You need to start LOCALLY! So, that doesn't mean move to South Carolina, just

food for thought for the future. Why stay local at the beginning? You know which communities are the best, which schools are best, the areas of high crime rates, where the shopping centers are. Start with the classified ads or place your own ad. That also means the classified ads on the internet. As well, you can post your ads in supermarkets and laundromats.

The longer the property is on the market typically the more room there is for negotiation. Call the city tax assessor to find the name, address and telephone number of that individual's home to contact. Look in the paper. Make a list of friends, neighbors, and co-workers and ask them if they have seen any properties that fit your descriptions. Call realtors. You might have to look at 30 deals before you find one good one but the key is to be aware of possibilities.

The Perfect Deal

There is never a perfect deal and opportunities can be lost by waiting for the perfect time, condition, or other circumstances. Also, many deals are within 20 miles of your home. The key is to start looking. Please be aware that it can be long, exhausting hours of work, but over time you will get better at it, and you will not need as much time. This is why the mentality part was emphasized in the beginning of this book. It is amazing how many opportunities you find when you start looking with an open mind that you would have never noticed before.

Additionally, keep an eye open for trends. The reason why real estate did so well from 2003 to 2007 was because people were tired of losing money in the stock market, so they shifted from investing in stocks into real estate. Low interest rates are a good sign of a time where it's prudent to buy real estate. People can afford a home that, if interest rates were high, they might not have been able to afford. Look towards the stock market as an indicator of things to come.

The stock market will do well even though the country might still be in a recession because the market looks about six months into the future to indicate what might be happening. It is a leading indicator. So, if the economy is improving, people start to buy houses again.

In a recession, people tend to rent more. In which case, hold on to the property until the up-market, then sell it and in an up-market, buy and flip it. Great bargains can be found in a down market. So, you can purchase your real estate depending on what the economic trend is. Call the Chamber of Commerce and look at the migration of people in your area, is it a growing neighborhood? Find out what the median income is. Read your local newspaper for trends. Go to your planning development board and see what is coming in the future. Moving companies are great sources to find out the trends of an area. How many new developments are being built? Look up online your area's home sales and some statistics. It is so much easier today than in the past. Thank goodness for the computer. The point is when you do the things above, you can see a trend and capitalize on it.

People want to know what exactly that may be, but I cannot exactly tell you as trends change like the tides. If there are plans for a new major development or a large company coming to your area, interest rates will be cut, and your county will grow because people are migrating out of the city to your area because home prices are too high where they used to live. Do you think that this is a good sign for real estate? Same thing if the large company moves out of your area and takes all their jobs with it. Sometimes it is simply common sense. Experience will make these common sense decisions easier for you in the future. In a downward market, renting is the key, but be AWARE, getting the right price for a home is always the right strategy regardless of any market. Also, flipping homes is not always the right answer during the bull market of real estate. There will always be new highs in real estate. Contact the FDIC, IRS and FSLIC for a printed list of distressed properties.

An excellent deal for the first time homebuyer or investor is to buy a two family home and rent out one half.

Another great idea I heard is to pass out your business cards and give referral fees of up to $1,000 if someone finds you the right property. It is one of the last things you can do in any business to pay people for helping you. In my business, a financial planner, for example you cannot give any one person over $100. So make a goal of passing out 2-3 business cards a day, and believe me, when people see the $1,000 referral fee they will be more conscious of finding opportunities. Mass mail works nicely here for people who are in default or in the process of foreclosures; trust me these people are looking for solutions and are desperate.

Look for people who have moved out of the area, vacation homes, tax problems, money problems, divorce, partnership breakups, estate problems, or health issues. These are the people who need your help. Try to pick an area five miles in your area and become an expert about it.

The key as in anything in life is to work on solutions that benefit all parties on every deal. If you keep this in mind, you will be blessed and business will continue to come your way.

So, if you are serious about real estate – here is your assignment: A word of warning, just doing one thing is not good enough! All must come into play to find that one deal. If you close, flip, or find three to five real estate deals a year, for most people who have real estate as part of their wealth planning deals, this is all they need to build a substantial amount of wealth - especially if you do this for 10 years (30-50 properties). Do the following in your area: 1. Join Real Estate investment groups. 2. Run your own paid ads 3. Hand out at least three business cards a week with the referral fee on the back of your cards. 4. Contact all friends. 5. Call your contacts. 6. Target three banks to work with in their foreclosure departments. 7. Call three realtors and develop partnerships. 8. Go and look up properties at your local courthouse 9. Contact two attorneys who deal with BK's and specialize in real estate.

Do all 9 of these exercises and I promise that leads will flow in the future.

The key here is to take a look at all these factors I mentioned above and plan accordingly.

The most important thing I can tell you about real estate is to have your eyes open. When you find a house, typically a house that needs work in a nice neighborhood, do not be afraid to think creatively. You never know what type of situation the owner is in. The reason why we spend so much time on the mentality section is because it takes courage to buy properties in distress. When a house looks perfect, you do not really have as many worries as seeing a house that needs a major touch up. If you can get past your worries and see the future potential, these properties have the largest potential for profit because you typically buy them at a discount and thus you have a larger potential for profit. It does not cost anything to make a bid. This is actually a good way of practicing.

ALWAYS have a clause in your contract that will allow you out of your deal such as subject to buyer's attorney's approval or offer subject to buyer's final inspection of property prior to closing. Also, many states have a buyer's remorse code that will allow you to back out of a deal within a certain number of days.

It is vital that you understand what a good deal really is. I cannot begin to tell you about people who invest in real estate who come into my office and think their investment in real estate is a great deal because most people really do not know how to properly calculate a return. If one purchases a property for $240,000 and puts down 20% ($40,000) and takes out a mortgage for the remaining $200,000 at 5% for 30 years, then let's say it is sold in 10 years for $400,000. After 10 years the mortgage balance would be $163,078. Most people subtract the mortgage balance and down payment from the sale price and divide by the down payment to determine the investment return. In this example, it would be as follows: ($400,000-$40,000-$163,078) = $196,922 return over 10 years.

The problem is that most people do not keep track of what they spend on repairs, additions, or improvements. Let's say, in this example, that one spent

$30,000 on repairs and improvements. Also, the sale requires a realtor who collects 6% of the sale price ($24,000), and tax on the gain which could be around $3,000. This doesn't even consider insurance. The real return on investment is $196,922-$30,000-$24,000-$3,000 = $139,922.

The most important thing to remember is that the bank gave you most of the money, so what it really comes down to is what you actually paid out of your pocket.

Here is how you simply evaluate a deal. Find a purchase price that is 10% less than what typical properties are going for. How do you know? You pull up comparables in the neighborhood. These are houses with the same size and condition. Find out the approximate closing costs, and the financing to obtain it, which requires how much money to put down. You will need to know the repairs to be made, and how much you can rent the home for, including a month-long vacancy. Additionally, you will need to know the cost for managing the place, and the expenses you will be paying for (like a utility bill, etc.). The real return comes from the amount you net compared to the amount of money down. If you make $125 a month profit, that equals a $1,500 return plus 5% appreciation on a $100,000 building of $5,000 and tax deductions that let's say are offset from additional expenses on a $23,000 down payment. This equals a 28% return. $6,500/$23,000. Not bad.

Instead of paying a realtor a commission of 6%, I offered a person $2,000 over their asking price of $200,000. But instead of giving them the money up front, I assumed the first mortgage and paid the $42,000 of their equity in a note with a great rate of 8% for 10 years. (CD's were paying 3%) The client got over the full asking price, a rate of 8% which was great at the time, and did not have to pay $14,000 in commissions to a realtor. This can also help out the realtor. A client wanted more than what they can actually get for the house because they needed the money.

So, in speaking to the realtor, using common sense, I told him that he can get his commissions, but the client can walk away with the money he needs, and he did not have to worry about the house sitting on the market for a long period of time. How? Instead of paying the realtor the $15,000 in commissions up front, I gave him a secured note for $15,000 for five years with interest of 6%. If he did not take the deal, people were not going to buy a house above what the other homes were selling. So, he could continue to waste his time and effort, but the owner needed the money and would not settle for less, so no one would win. I assumed the mortgage, promised the realtor my next listing, and everyone got what they wanted.

You do not have to do this with equity alone. You can use this same technique with almost any debts. Medical bills are another good example that you can use with this technique. Another awesome example of using creative thinking is a client of mine who bought a commercial building brand new. He made an offer that he would buy the building with the stipulation that it would be fully rented by the time he bought it and that the renters will pay two month's rent deposits. The seller agreed. He then used the $23,000 he collected from the rent deposits as money that he was short on for the down payment.

As stated before, anyone can own a house if they can afford the rental payments. How? A lease to own option. Make sure that part of your rent payment goes towards the down payment of your home.

Another idea is that if you pick up a house below market value and it could be an excellent potential flip, then get the down payment from a private investor. I once borrowed a $50,000 down payment from a private investor, gave him a rate of 10% until I sold it and gave him an extra $15,000 on top of the note when I sold the home. How could that investor say no? Especially if you show the investor what you could sell the home for.

Also, when looking to borrow money, you could do so with a margin loan against your stock portfolio, with rates favorable and you picking up a great property; this could also be a way of getting the cash you need to buy an investment property.

A rule of thumb when buying a property is to add the words to your contract "and/or assigns." This way you can sell the property without actually purchasing the property. I always tell almost everyone that I meet with that I am selling property before I am about to close, and the reason is that people might be interested in buying the property. For example, I found a property worth about $150,000 and was going to buy it for $108,000. However, when speaking to a business associate about the property, he said he always wanted to buy rental properties. I sold it to him for $118,000, well below market price, which he was grateful for and pocketed $10,000 without ever taking possession of the property. You can also advertise in newspapers about some of these properties and actually sell them to someone without taking possession of the property.

Protecting Your Real Estate

Almost all the properties I own are different LLC's. So if someone slips on one of my properties, they cannot sue me and take my other properties because they are different entities, or even worse, sue me personally. Please remember that people abuse the legal system and protection today is necessary. Think about the famous case of a woman who won over $2 million because SHE spilled the coffee on herself, or the burglar who won thousands of dollars because he suffered an injury while burglarizing a home. Remember the more units, the more profits.

Deferring taxes on real estate. When you sell a property and intend on buying a new property for the same or greater value, use a 1031 exchange so that no taxes are due. Also, investments made in real estate for a business purpose can have a tax advantage through the use of depreciation. You could also depreciate a property quickly through the use of advanced depreciation techniques which will depreciate a property quicker, as fast as 5 years, thus giving you greater tax deductions when you need it. Instead of depreciating a property over 39 years, you could do it all over 5 years.

If you want to pay your house off early simply pay your payment to the mortgage company every week instead of once a month as long as the full payment is there by your due date. This will cut a few years off your mortgage because it does not give the interest time to compound. This is especially a great idea to do when you first start making mortgage payments. You can include an extra payment towards your mortgage monthly or even make an extra payment a year, perhaps when you get your income tax return back. A rule of thumb is to try not to include your points on your mortgage. I would rather see you borrow from your 401(k) plan than do this.

Do not forget to take advantage of the government; meaning the SBA (Small Business Association). www.govloans.com will help you get started. SBA will help give you grants - which is free money or loans and great rates. Go to www.sba.gov/SBIR/indexsbir-strr.html and you might be eligible. This does not just include real estate but ANY business you want to start. Do not forget about your private foundations as well. The key is you cannot be lucky unless you take the chance to become lucky.

Warnings

If you own real estate outside of your current state you will go through probate again in the state where the real estate is located. A trust can help with this issue.

Special Warning about Commercial Real Estate: For most people stay away from it. There is literally no protection at all. Let me tell you my story...

I had a great relationship with a local community bank. They were taken over by a large bank. I took out an adjustable loan in which my rate fell down to 3.25%. The bank did not want to be in my area or have a loan this low on their books. So they called in my loan meaning that the full payment was due on my mortgage even though I had a 20 year balloon. The bank stated that my payment was due on the 1st and I paid on the 3rd. So, technically they stated I was late. (There is no grace period on commercial loans.) This immoral bank used this as an excuse to have my loan due immediately. So, I had to find another bank. The problem was that I had an ex firm I cleared through withhold a large amount of money, which made me 30 days late on some bills, thus damaging my credit and incurring a lot higher rates.

By the way if I default, they attach your personal home - that is called a personal guarantee! With residential property, if you default on one, especially if it is a LLC, then they cannot attach your personal home. If you have a business, that is ok but owning several commercial properties, for most people, I say stay away.

Lastly, for those who might be in trouble with real estate. There are many loan modification programs out there through your banks. Trust me, banks do not want to own real estate. There are modifications on 40 year loans at close to 5% for those who ask and want a lower payment. This is not refinancing, it is adjusting the existing mortgage to make it more affordable - mostly at zero cost to you. Ask for forbearance – a suspension of payments for a few months. Go to www.hud.gov to find free services that might help you.

Protecting Your Assets

I hate to go into statistics, but if you have any success and are thinking about marriage, a prenuptial agreement is almost necessary.

Defined benefit plans like 401(k) plans can be exempt from bankruptcies and sometimes lawsuits. 401(k)'s up to an unlimited amount and IRA's up to a million. Also exempt are annuities, and your primary home through the Homestead Act from a state exemption standpoint. So, use them if it is appropriate to protect your assets. (Check your state's rules. New Jersey, for example, offers no protection for your house.)

Transferring assets to a spouse and thinking you are protected… Wrong, especially if the spouse's income was used to purchase the asset, if they benefited from it, and have control over the asset. "Control" is the big word. A creditor has a strong claim against the "substance of the arrangement." Also, transferring your home to your children while you are still alive isn't a great solution. Your children just inherited your cost basis, so when they sell the home, they pay the difference of what you paid for the house and what the market value of the house is upon your death. You bought it for $100k and you died when it was worth $500k. $400k is taxable to them. Waiting upon your death to gift the house gives the children a step-up in basis and they pay zero capital gains tax. (There will be other taxes.) Most people do this because they have no Long Term Care, but as stated earlier, there is a 5 year look back period where the government can go back and attack those assets. How do you protect your home? You are not going to like it, and it is the opposite of what 99% of the population wants to have = a mortgage. Take out as much equity as possible from your home and place the assets in an asset protection trust, which can then be invested. The key is to get a better return than the mortgage rate you are paying which is very attractive as I write this with loans as low as 2-4%.

There is so much information on trusts and many people are selling them where in most cases it is not necessary. Revocable trust assets are fully attachable to a creditor. They offer no asset protection. Irrevocable trusts are great for asset protection but you cannot make any changes once you establish the trust. A great clause in the irrevocable trust for your children is the spendthrift clause which could protect your assets from the beneficiaries' creditors. People also think that you can lose control when transferring assets. Not true, you can gift 100% of your assets to your children and still have control over your assets. Also, the tax can be transferred to your children. You can also still have the income from the asset. Lease backs with an LLC can be very effective.

FLP (Family Limited Partnership) and LLC. A creditor cannot seize the assets in these entities if they are going after you. They can only file a charging order. This means they are allowed to get the distributions that would have been paid by the debtor. The business can still operate normally. You can still keep control and you can still pay yourself and your spouse a reasonable salary for running the FLP. The thing to remember about FLP and LLC is that a dangerous asset should be owned by an LLC. In a FLP, a general partner could be personally liable.

Recap Section: Getting Started

Find out what you want to do. Sounds simple but this stalls most people. If you can not get past this part then you are in trouble. Make a commitment then to create a goal. The biggest problem is that most people limit what they think they can achieve. They might say open a restaurant but limit their thinking. That is what happened to the McDonald brothers. Ray Kroc saw the vision of expanding the restaurants nationwide. We are truly limited by our own thinking.

After creating the goal make a list of steps you need to reach that goal: the resources, the people, etc. Also, make a list of all potential obstacles. Once again, why we spent all that time on the mentality part. If you want to dream big, then the obstacles will be great as well. That is fine if you do not know what all those steps are, as long as you write down what you believe to know.

The goals you cannot handle on your own? Guess what? That's right - partner with someone.

People want to make these steps harder than they are. They are not. As Nike says, "just do it."

Giving Back

I do not know why this is the case but you have to give to get. It is just a spiritual law that seems to always be the case.

Let's clear the excuses that I do not have anything to give. When people think of giving, right away they think of money. There are other ways to give such as your time, chipping in and giving a hand, saying "thank you" and smiling. Please make sure that when you give, you feel good about it. I could give to a school but instead I give out two scholarships to college every year, I get to make a speech, and more importantly, get to watch the excitement of not only the student but the parents when I announce their names, and that, in itself, always makes me feel good and puts a smile on my face. The bottom line is that giving always helps you get what you want.

In the Bible, it also states that every true need will be given to you. In Proverbs 11:24-25, it states that those who give will receive even more back than what was given. This is pretty amazing. You have a powerful weapon available to you by just giving generously. The gentleman who started the successful Templeton Fund wisely stated, "Tithing always gives the greatest return on your investment."

They say that giving away 10% is important. Some people call this "tithing." In fact, by giving away 10%, you actually receive more because it says that you can be trusted with the monies that you receive. When you do give, it needs to feel good, which does not always mean giving your money to the church or an institution.

The key to giving is to feel good about it. When I give away the scholarship to my old high school, this makes me feel really good inside. Giving could mean simple things such as leaving a 40% tip instead of 15%, giving money to a friend, giving your clothes to a charity, tipping your garbage man. It is through your feeling that you know where your money should go.

I heard a lesson that I still struggle with today, which is to tithe first, then you become rich. I always thought that you become rich, and THEN you tithe. However, you do not always have to start out at 10%. Start with less and then work your way up.

Unfortunately, by not following this rule, sometimes "bad luck" could follow such as speeding tickets, fewer bargains, or paying more for items than you want. In short, I believe it is a way for the universe to see if we could be trusted with money, or that we can use money for the benefit of the general good of the world. Giving could be the key to receiving. God wants to give you everything, so when you give, He will reward you for what He does on a daily basis. It is stated that for every dollar you give, 10 times that amount comes back to you. That's a pretty good deal. Remember that you are not giving for others' benefit, you are giving for the benefit for yourself. By not giving, wealth will decline, relationships will deteriorate, and remember that you are being tested.

Spending to save people or others is like playing God, it comes between you and God. This is the most difficult lesson of them all, especially if your sister has fallen on bad times, she is behind on her mortgage, or she is buying used clothes for her children. You do not know why God has given her hard times. Perhaps He is trying to force change in their lives, for her to relocate, go back to school, start her own business so that she can finally prosper, or for her to go to therapy to change her behavior.

Give for no reason. Another warning is to not hoard money. Saving for a rainy day is exactly what you are telling the universe you want – a rainy day outside of emergency money, which is 3 months reserve if both couples are working, and 6 months with one employed. Remember your subconscious will produce exactly what you are thinking or afraid of happening. An important trait that humans strive for is to find purpose in life or meaning to their existence. This will help you in determining where your money goes to at your passing.

SETTING GOALS

One of the things that I have done is follow the model set by Jim Carrey. I wrote a check out for $5 million dollars and kept it in my wallet.

With this goal in mind, you can reach for the sky. There are no limits to where you can go. One of my favorite quotes is by Abraham Lincoln that says, "Things may come to those who wait, but only the things left by those who hustle."

PEOPLE WHO HAVE DONE IT

The most powerful thing we can do when we are confronted with adversity is to try again. It will serve us well through life. Perseverance is the #1 quality of all great success stories…

- Did you know that Thomas Edison was a first grade drop out? His teacher thought he was mentally challenged.

- Walt Disney went to 300 banks before he received his loan to build Disney World. He also was broke, and when he arrived in Hollywood, he had less than $50 in his wallet and a few items of clothing to his name.

- Michael Landon – flunked out of college his freshman year and was actually homeless at one point.

- How about a man's dream of becoming a professional soccer player. He gets into an accident where he can never play again. He picks up a guitar and decides to write and sing songs. His name is Julio Iglesias.

- John D. Rockefeller was a ten cents an hour bookkeeper. He accumulated the largest percent of the United States gross national product than any American including today.

- How about a woman living on welfare, divorced, getting rejected by over 12 publishers, and did not even have a computer. She wrote a book called *Harry Potter* and her name was J.K Rowling.

- Beethoven – his teacher called him a hopeless composer and said he did not have good technique.

In closing, does that mean that you are balanced and that you will have no insecurities? Not true. In a study by a private banker of 2,000 households with a net worth of $38 million or more, 64% still failed financially.

At the end, it does not make a difference what your current circumstances are. In John 7:24, the Bible states, "Judge not according to the appearance." It is not where you are but where you are going. Through a belief system and action you will be that person you wish to become.

www.ingramcontent.com/pod-product-compliance
Lightning Source LLC
Chambersburg PA
CBHW061509180526
45171CB00001B/101